Creating
Sacred Space
with
Feng Shui

Creating Sacred Space with Feng Shui

KAREN KINGSTON

BROADWAY BOOKS

New York

BROADWAY

This book was originally published in 1996 in Great Britain by Judy Piatkus (Publishers) Ltd. It is here reprinted by arrangement with Judy Piatkus (Publishers) Ltd.

Library of Congress Cataloging-in-Publication Data
Kingston, Karen.
Creating sacred space with Feng Shui / by Karen Kingston.
p.   cm.
Includes index.
ISBN 0-553-06916-0
1. Feng Shui.   I. Title.
BF1779.F4K56   1997
133.3′33—dc20   96-9303
CIP

Book design by Claire Vaccaro
Illustrations by Susan Ure Reid

Contents

Acknowledgments

My heartfelt thanks and gratitude:

To Rai, my husband, who is Balinese, for creating space in our relationship for this book to be written. Thank you for your sweetness of heart and incredible love.

To my mother, Jean Kingston, for giving me the freedom to always be myself and to my father, Frank Kingston, for instilling in me at an early age that where there's a will, there's a way.

To my best friend, Leigh Mollett, for teaching me compassion and believing in me until I learned how to believe in myself.

To Keith Meehan, for your steadfast friendship and generosity of home and heart.

To Denise Linn, for spontaneously giving me your microphone in 1991 to tell two hundred participants in your workshop about the wonders of Space Clearing! Your love, support, and encouragement have played a very large part in bringing this book into being.

To Gina Lazenby, for having the foresight, dedication, and stamina to create the organization to launch my workshops into the world. Thank you for all your work and your valued friendship.

To Sean Milligran, Leonard Orr, William Spear, and Graham Wilson. You all know the part you have played in bringing this book into being. I thank you with all my heart.

To Anne Lawrance, the most lovable, competent, unflustered editor a budding new author could wish to have, and to Susan Ure Reid for your exquisite illustrations, created with so much love.

To Roger Coghill, many thanks for checking the content of, and making contributions to, my chapter on electromagnetic stress.

To unseen helpers, all my teachers (especially Peter, wherever you are now) and all my wonderful Balinese friends who have unknowingly contributed to this book by sharing their wisdom and way of life with me.

To all who have attended and participated in my workshops for your enthusiasm, contributions, and invaluable feedback.

To all who have invited me into your homes for private consultations. It is always a privilege and illuminating experience to be asked to work on such an intimate level in someone's personal space.

Finally, I acknowledge all of you who read this book and use the material to improve the quality of your life. I have enjoyed writing it tremendously and hope that you derive equally as much pleasure, insight, and benefit from reading it and applying it to your own life.

Foreword

In the spring of 1991, I was scheduled to lead a Past Lives Practitioners course at the Royal Horticultural Halls in Victoria, London. There were more than two hundred participants in the training, so the organizers had arranged for the seminar to be simultaneously conducted on two floors, with my voice being transmitted with loudspeakers to an upper floor. I arrived at the halls early to prepare both rooms and to meet with the individuals who were going to be assisting me at the workshop.

Whenever I give a seminar, I try to have a number of healers and therapists assist me by surrounding the periphery of the room. This creates a sense of comfort and love for the participants. I find that within this wonderful safe space people can go more deeply and powerfully into meditation. That morning I was fortunate to have a special woman named Karen Kingston, who was a well-known London therapist, come to assist. Although I was aware of Karen's abilities as a therapist, I wasn't aware of her Space Clearing abilities, a talent I learned about in a very dramatic way.

After the lower room was prepared for the arrival of the participants, I went upstairs to check on the upper floor. I was completely dismayed by the feeling in the room. The energy felt thick and heavy and dull. I was called away from the room for a few minutes. When I walked back in, I stopped abruptly in amazement.

"What happened in here?" I cried out. The room was empty with the exception of a small group of assistants, who started at my resounding voice. I had cried out because I was startled by the profound change in the energy. The room no longer felt heavy and depressing. Even though none of the physical objects had been moved, the entire room sparkled with light and energy. It was quite remarkable. Karen very quietly stepped forward from the group and explained that she had been Space Clearing the room.

"The energy shift is incredible," I told her.

She looked surprised and said, "I've never met anyone before who had the sensitivity to register the changes in a room so instantly, especially when I am only halfway through it!" In that moment there was a deep recognition between us as we realized that we had each met someone else who shared the same unusual skills. So began a rich and loving friendship that continues to this day.

The next morning I invited Karen to speak about Space Clearing at my seminar. The depth of her knowledge and the warmth of her personality captivated the audience. Even with her voice she is able to create a space filled with beautiful energy. Since then we have worked together on numerous occasions, and Karen has gone on to establish herself as an international seminar leader and top Feng Shui and Space Clearing consultant, as well as a prolific writer. Her teachings have been received all over the globe. When Karen told me that she would be writing this book, I was delighted. She has a style that is unique, so much of it being influenced by her life in Bali.

Karen's book is about using the ancient art of Feng Shui and Space Clearing to create sacred space in your home and workplace, which will allow you to create more health, wealth, and happiness in your life. Feng Shui is about the natural flow of energy that is in all things. The words *feng* and *shui* translate literally as "wind" and "water," which are the two forces of natural energy, or chi, that flow through the heavens and the earth. Chi is the interconnection to all that is in the universe. It is the cosmic breath of energy that runs through all things. Poor design, awkward placement, and clogged energy in buildings can inhibit anything you try to do while living or working in that place. Feng Shui and Space Clearing teach us how to balance and harmonize chi to create balance and harmony in our lives.

Karen is an exceptional teacher and practitioner who has found a way to bring the oriental art of Feng Shui into modern Western society. She understands very well the expression "being in the flow," which means everything seems to fall naturally into place. When you are in the right place at the right time everything goes well for you. For many years people have believed that this is fate. However, by practicing what is in this book you can learn how to be in harmony with your environment so that you can be at the right place and in control of your destiny. I know from years of personal experience what remarkable results creating sacred space can produce in people's lives.

In ancient China it is said, "If there is harmony in the home, there will be order in the nation. If there is order in the nation, there will be peace in the world." As we approach the end of the millennium, there has never been a more important time in the history of our planet for this to be a focus in our lives. Karen's book contains vital information that will help you create ease and flow in your life's journey, to allow you to remember who you are and do what you are here to do. This in turn can lead to a more healthy and harmonious planet, like a pebble dropped in a still pool whose ripples reach to the farthest shore.

DENISE LINN
Author of *Sacred Space*

PART ONE

Space
Clearing

1.

My Feng Shui
Journey

EARLY BEGINNINGS

One evening in 1978, I was driving over to visit a couple of friends who had just moved into a new apartment when an idea occurred to me that—although I did not know it then—was to change the course of my life.

I arrived on their doorstep and explained to them what I had in mind. Rather than have them show me around their new home, I asked them to allow me to explore their place blindfolded.

For a couple of years I had been developing my senses, and especially my ability to read energies with my hands, to detect and translate the electromagnetic pulsations that emanate from living beings and also from so-called "inanimate" objects. I usually describe it as being able to read information with my hands in the same way as I might read a book with my eyes. I had practiced a lot in my own home and public buildings but had never tried it in anyone else's home before, and never blindfolded.

They were as interested as I was to try this little experiment, so they hunted out a thick black silk scarf and tied it tightly around my eyes. Then, starting at the front door, we began our journey around the apartment, following the inside perimeter of the space.

I led the way, moving very slowly down the corridor and into the front room. With my hands acting as antennae, I followed the contours of the walls, furniture, and other objects, never quite touching them, just sensing the energy emanating from them.

The first thing I discovered was that I could mostly tell which pieces of furniture belonged to my friends and which belonged to the landlord. The pieces belonging to my friends had a warm, familiar energy to them, whereas those belonging to the landlord had a much duller, more ponderous vibration.

We all started to get excited. "See if you can tell us what pictures we have on the wall," my friends challenged me.

This took a while longer, but I discovered I could feel very precisely where there were pictures on the wall, and when I fine-tuned I was able to tell them what color the pictures were and sometimes the content of the pictures too. They had several framed photographs of people around the apartment, and I was able to name some of them.

"Let's see what else you can do," my friends encouraged me. They were totally fascinated now. They asked me to sense which decorative objects were theirs, and we were all dismayed when my accuracy rating fell dramatically with this. At first we couldn't figure it out, and then they realized that many of their decorative objects were antiques that had had previous owners, and so were imbued with the energy of the previous owners too. It was this that had confused me.

This gave me the idea to go around the space again, sensing in a completely different way. This time I focused on what had happened in the space before they had come to live there. Now we were really heading into the unknown because none of us knew anything about the history of the apartment. I felt I was guessing, but I described some of the vibrations I was picking up as best I could. One very strong signal was what I could only describe at the time as "mental hardness." I also registered painful aches in my bones, especially my finger joints.

I spent the whole evening going around the apartment sensing the different energies, and I didn't take the blindfold off until I went out of the front door and said goodbye. A week later I got an excited phone call to tell me that they had checked with the landlord and discovered that the previous tenant had lived there for twenty years and had been a very stubborn old man with severe arthritis, especially in his hands!

L A T E R   D E V E L O P M E N T S

The experience of that evening really gave me the impetus to go on and develop my skills even more. I continued to develop my ability to sense energies through my hands and skin and also to see, hear, smell, and taste on an energetic level. I also developed my intuition and studied all the major . divinatory arts, such as palmistry, astrology, tarot, numerology, graphology, and so on. I learned how to heal through color, music, toning, crystals, and many other means. Using a unique channeling technique, I was able to connect directly to the core essence of, and study the music, dance, and spiritual ceremonials of, many different planetary cultures. I became very skilled at getting myself out of the way so that I could channel this information clearly and powerfully.

As my ability to read energies in buildings developed, I began to realize that a lot of it was unsavory and undesirable. In particular, I wanted my own home to be as free from other influences as possible. It was therefore a natural progression to learn ways to cleanse and clear the energy of buildings, and I called these techniques "Space Clearing," which seemed to describe the process very aptly. It became fundamental to my life to clear any space before I lived in it and then to create and maintain high-level atmospheres in that place.

Something I began to practice a few years down the line was what I now know as "the art of placement." I learned that when I arranged things in a certain way in relation to other things and the spatial dimensions around them, something amazing happened with the energy. I began to use it to create incredible results in my life. Whenever something wasn't going quite right, I would go home and rearrange or change my furniture and decorative objects until suddenly I registered a "click" in the energy fields, as if everything had suddenly come into alignment. After that, everything worked better in my life. Later, as I developed this even more, I acquired a reputation among my friends for my ability to manifest the seemingly impossible in my life again and again and again.

All this was immense fun, a fantastic voyage of discovery. I played with the energies and tried out new ideas to see what worked and what didn't. I learned how to change atmospheres, how to soup them up, and how to tone them down. People would come to visit me and would stop in their tracks and say, "Wow! What an amazing place!" or "What a lovely feeling there is here!" and they never wanted to leave when it was time to go. It happened so often that I knew for a fact that I was producing tangible results.

After I had been doing all this for about ten years, a friend of mine put a book under my nose, which was a huge illustrated volume containing a chapter on something I had never heard of, called Feng Shui. He said to me, "Look at this! The Chinese were on to all this stuff about three thousand years before you!" I read the chapter with interest, but most of it was oriental gobbledygook and didn't make a lot of sense to me at that time. However, it was wonderful to know that some research had already been done in this area, and later when I came to understand it more, it was great for me to check out and augment the work that I had already developed by myself, working purely from the energy standpoint.

As the years went by, I continued to develop new skills. I trained as a bodyworker. I found that I could run my hands over people's bodies several inches away from their skin, read memories and traumas stored in the body tissues, and help people clear them. I learned how to work with the breath and became a professional rebirther, teaching people how to use the breath to find their own answers from within. I became skilled at knowing what a person was feeling and experiencing simply from the way they took in energy by breathing, and I could help them release long-standing energy blocks by becoming conscious of them. I combined body harmony, reiki, other forms of bodywork, and metaphysical counseling into my rebirthing sessions to obtain very powerful results.

During the time I was working with the energy of people, I was also progressing my skills working with the energy of places, never expecting that anyone would ever actually be interested in learning about it. It has been very exciting for me to be at the leading edge of the recent explosion of interest in the subject in the Western world and to find that all my skills suddenly have a use and a value to others.

DISCOVERING BALI

In 1990 my studies took another leap forward when I discovered Bali, a tiny island in the Indonesian archipelago. This vibrant, spiritual culture is one of the best examples of a people living in perfect harmony with their natural surroundings, and they have the most highly developed purification ceremonies I have encountered anywhere on earth. I fell totally in love with the place, spent most of the next three years there, and have continued to live there for half of each year ever since.

I discovered a natural aptitude for the Indonesian language and then started learning Balinese, a wonderfully descriptive and incredibly complex language with three levels, umpteen dialects, and no dictionaries, known to only a handful of westerners. Knowing this language really started to open doors for me, especially with the older priests and shamans who speak hardly a word of Indonesian, having left school long before the study of this language was introduced. There will be a lot more about Bali and the results of my work with these priests and shamans as this book unfolds.

STARTING TO TEACH

For a long time I resisted teaching Space Clearing to anyone except a few close friends because I didn't want to get labeled "cranky" or "weird." Then I started teaching a metaphysical workshop called "Create the Life You Really Want," and I noticed something very interesting: people got good results from the workshop, but the people who got the best results were personal friends whom I had taught how to clear energies in their own homes.

It was the incident that Denise Linn describes in the foreword to this book that really prompted me to start teaching more people how to do Space Clearing. We hardly knew each other at that time, but the very next day Denise created some time in her workshop and asked me to teach what

I knew about Space Clearing to all the people who were taking her Past Lives Practitioners course. Afterward I was swamped by people telling me how exciting the information was and asking me to do private consultations in their homes. I was amazed and surprised and delighted all at once. Denise encouraged me to start teaching my own workshops and even got me started by recommending me to her own organizers in England and Australia. I now teach Feng Shui, Space Clearing, and workshops on related topics all over the world.

CONTINUING EXPANSION

The name "Feng Shui" originates in China, but over the years I have discovered that every culture in the world has a form of Feng Shui and also the branch of Feng Shui concerned with clearing and consecrating spaces, which I call Space Clearing. I have adapted techniques from wherever I have found something useful—from China, Japan, India, America, Great Britain, from many European and Middle Eastern countries and, of course, from Bali.

Some of the information I have come across in books and different cultures has been conflicting, but because I work from the energy standpoint all the time, it has been very easy for me to discern which bits work and which bits don't, and which bits can be adapted to Western life and which bits don't fit so well. My life has been an exciting journey of discovery and a process of researching, checking, and refining my findings.

When I do a Feng Shui or Space Clearing consultation, the first thing I do is go around the inside perimeter of the space and take an energy reading on many different levels. Then it's a matter of working with the person or people who live or work there at whatever depth they want me to. I remember one woman was so pleased to discover my abilities that the one-hour consultation she had originally booked me for developed into a seven-hour in-depth reading of virtually every room of her four-story mansion. She was a very caring mother who had had a string of difficult problems with her adult children. When she discovered my ability to fine-tune and read the energy of her home, she asked me to go into each room in the house and tell her exactly what vibrations were stored in the walls, furniture, and decorative objects. I was able to tell her about each of her children, about their characters, their inner struggles, their higher aspirations, and what help each of them would most benefit from.

People often ask me if I think my skills are unique. I think I have a natural empathy and passion for working with energy, but the rest is the result of years and years of perfecting my abilities. Since I began teaching the information contained in this book in my workshops, many people have discovered that they too can learn to read energies and can Feng Shui and Space Clear their homes and workplaces. I have formulated ways of teaching this material so that, without any previous training, people can go and begin to use it in their own lives immediately. Letters and phone calls arrive daily telling me of exciting things that have happened as a result of doing this. Now I have put the material into written form so that many more people can access and use it.

WHAT THIS BOOK IS ABOUT

This book is in five parts:

- Part One forms an introduction to the subjects of Feng Shui and Space Clearing, and contains a 21-step guide to teach you how to Space Clear your own home;

- Part Two explains the basic Space Clearing procedures in more detail and goes through all the different methods of purification you can use so that you can formulate your own ceremonies;

- Part Three looks at deeper levels of consecrating space and creating sacredness in your life;

- Part Four opens up awareness of another aspect of energy in the form of electromagnetic stress, from both natural and human-made sources;

- Part Five teaches you how to apply the Feng Shui art of placement in your own home, using cures and enhancements such as mirrors and crystals.

I recommend that you use the book in the order it is presented. The Space Clearing and consecration techniques in the first three sections and the information about electromagnetism in the fourth section will enable you to obtain excellent results when using the information about the Feng Shui art of placement in the final section.

Throughout most of this book, I refer to your home as the building to which you will be applying the techniques. Of course all the techniques can be applied equally well to your workspace and any other buildings you occupy.

2.

What Is Feng Shui?

For many people who have studied visualization and other methods of manifesting changes in their lives, Feng Shui and Space Clearing open up huge exciting new vistas. When you "put your house in order," it is like discovering a whole army of helpers you never realized were at your disposal.

The information in this book will take you on a journey of self-discovery by teaching you how to read the symbolism and energy of your home and how to change it for the better. By adjusting and balancing the flow of energy within your home, you can powerfully and effectively influence the course of your life.

YOUR HOME

Think for a moment about your home. If you are reading this book at home, pause for a moment to look around you. How would you describe it? Is it elegant, untidy, welcoming, makeshift, grandiose, stark, functional . . . ?

Whatever your description, realize that what you are looking at is the outer manifestation of your inner self. Everything in your outer life—especially your home environment—mirrors your inner self. Conversely, everything in your home has an effect on you, from the smallest object to the largest design structure.

Most people are not even conscious of the huge effect their home and work environments has on them. They usually think of buildings as being something in the background, not realizing that they can help or hinder their progress substantially. They respond unconsciously without even knowing they are being affected.

A good Feng Shui practitioner can tell as much about you from reading your home as, say, an astrologer can tell from looking at your birthchart, a palmist can tell from reading your palm, or a graphologist can interpret from your handwriting. It is all there in your home to be seen and felt. It couldn't *not* be there, because it all came from you in the first place. On some level, consciously or unconsciously, you have chosen where you live, chosen everything in it, and positioned items wherever they are. It all has a significance and an effect. Your home is the living portrayal of everything you are and what is happening in your life.

EVERYTHING IS ALIVE

Understanding Feng Shui and Space Clearing begins with the awareness that each particle of creation is alive and filled with life force energy, filled with spirit and intelligence. Our homes are alive. The chairs we sit on are alive. The rings we wear on our fingers are alive. Their consciousness is different from ours, but they are conscious, and if you know how to listen, all things can speak to us and reveal their secrets.

All my life I have had a sense of the livingness of things. The idea is not new, of course. Animism is an integral part of most so-called "primitive" cultures in the world that still have their connection to universal consciousness. In Bali, animism blends with Balinese Hinduism to form the basis of their religious practices. All families own at least one sacred object, which is believed to have mystical powers.

This beautiful planet on which we live is not a dead lump of rock hurtling through space, destination unknown. It and everything on it is pulsating with energies. The Chinese call it *chi*, the Japanese call it *ki*, to the Hindus of India it is *prana*, to the Polynesians it is *mana*, and every other spiritual culture has its own name for it. We call it "spirit," "life force," or simply "energy."

One way that this can be seen is in the many different languages and cultural customs in the world, which arise in response to the different energies emanating from the earth. In some places you can journey just a few miles down the road and the local dialect changes completely, because the energy of the land is completely different.

Pure energy is all around us even though we may not see it until it affects something physical in our vicinity. Light cannot be seen until it illuminates something. Electricity cannot be seen, but we take it for granted every day when we turn on a light switch. Kirlian photography offers proof to the clinical Western mind of the energy fields emanating from all things. I once saw a Kirlian photograph of a slice of processed white bread alongside a slice of organic brown whole-grain bread. Around the white bread there was a flimsy excuse of an energy field, whereas the brown bread's emanation was strong, vital, and many times bigger. The difference was so startling that I have hardly ever eaten white bread since! Processed food loses so much of its vitality.

At its essence, Feng Shui is about living consciously on Mother Earth and enjoying the highest quality of life force possible for the human. It is the art of balancing, harmonizing, and enhancing the flow of natural energies, and since all things are permeated by these energies, this ancient art really can be applied in one way or another to everything we do.

FENG SHUI IN THE EAST

The name *Feng Shui* originates in China and translates as "wind and water." I use this term rather than any other because it has become the best-known name for this art in the Western world, but each traditional culture has its own name for it in its own language.

Feng Shui was first used in ancient China about three thousand years ago to determine the most auspicious sites for the tombs of ancestors in order to give them the best vantage to help their living descendants. Later it was used to site palaces, important government buildings, and monuments, until finally whole cities were designed and built according to Feng Shui principles.

Hong Kong is one such case in point, and its incredible prosperity is often cited as a prime example of Feng Shui's effectiveness. An estimated 90 percent of all properties in Hong Kong are built according to Feng Shui principles. The famous case of the Bank of China in Hong Kong, which was reportedly sued by neighboring businesses because the sharp angles of its seventy-story building impeded on them, is an example of how seriously Feng Shui is taken in the East. There is no doubt at all that the architect of this bank knew exactly what he was doing and deliberately designed a structure that sends arrowlike "killing chi" energy at its competitors. The immediate recourse of the occupants of surrounding buildings was to erect Feng Shui mirrors to attempt to reflect the dangerous energy back to its source—and commence litigation. This is an example of Feng Shui being used to manipulate energies rather than working for the highest good of all. The law of karma will ultimately be the great leveler, since what you give out is what you get back.

FENG SHUI IN THE WEST

In the early 1990s Feng Shui started to become popular in the United States, and—as with most things—it then slowly spread to the rest of the Western world. Today Feng Shui has become one of the "buzz" words of the latter half of the 1990s, and London is the Feng Shui capital of the Western world, with more workshops and training programs than in any other country.

Many people, when they first discover Feng Shui, say that it explains so many things they always knew deep down inside but never knew they knew! Most successful business entrepreneurs actually practice some form of Feng Shui without knowing they do. Sir William Lyons, chairman of Jaguar Cars, would always look for what he called the "light line" when looking at a newly designed car. The ideal light line was a smooth reflection of light along the side of a car from the front to the back, which in

Feng Shui terms would be a harmonious sweep of energy. He said the E-type Jaguar, the most popular and profitable car ever designed by Jaguar, had the best light line ever. The design of Anita Roddick's Body Shops, where walls of mirrors behind all the products symbolically double the profits, is another example of natural Feng Shui enhancement.

FENG SHUI AND SPACE CLEARING

Feng Shui comprises a vast body of knowledge, and to learn it in the East requires at least a thirty-year apprenticeship to a Feng Shui master. Most Western people have a very limited perception of this complex art, thinking it extends only as far as interior design and furniture placement, but this is merely one branch of Feng Shui. The art of cleansing and consecrating buildings (Space Clearing) is another important branch. Reading earth energies and choosing auspicious sites for buildings is another. A further branch deals with Feng Shui enhancements and cures. The study of Feng Shui also extends to orientation (a building's position in relation to the points of the compass or a significant topographical feature), directionology (the effects of moving in a particular compass direction), astrology, color, diet, medical diagnosis, and so on.

To become proficient in one branch of Feng Shui, even at today's enhanced speeds of learning, still requires several years of study and experience. However, there are some basic principles that can be taught relatively easily, and that is what I intend to do in this book. To begin with the study of Space Clearing makes this easier because it gives hands-on experience of how energy moves and affects us in our lives.

IMPROVING YOUR QUALITY OF LIFE

The whole premise of this book is that you want to learn how to have a happy, fulfilling, successful life. We are each of us spirit incarnate in a physical body on a physical planet, and one of our basic requirements is physical shelter. Playing "the shelter game" is part of the art of living in harmony with the physical universe, so even if you do not consider yourself to be a "spiritual" person, you may as well learn how to do it and get good at it if you are planning to be alive for any length of time at all! These are, in effect, some of the ground rules (pun intended) for living on Planet Earth.

The center of a Western home used to be the hearth fire or maybe the kitchen table—a meeting point for shared activities. Nowadays it is usually the television. If you doubt me, just see how the armchairs are all arranged in most living rooms. They are all angled toward the box in the corner. This has brought about a lessening in communication and community activities. It accentuates the feelings of separation that many people feel.

Many of us in the West have forgotten what life can be like. We feel separate and disconnected from the earth, disconnected from our environment, disconnected from each other, and disconnected from many of our basic sources of nourishment. There is so little sacredness in our lives.

When we are out of balance with our surroundings, we become physically, mentally, emotionally, and spiritually sick. We build buildings that make us sick and wonder why our lives seem to have no purpose. Now we are waking up to what Eastern cultures have known and practiced for centuries.

Feng Shui offers hope. It offers the means to reconnect and bring the sacredness back into our lives. In my travels around the world, I have consistently noticed that the East is looking to the West for what it does not have (materialism), and the West is looking to the East for what it does not have (spirituality). Feng Shui is a bridge between the two, which can be used by people from all nations, all religious backgrounds, and all walks of life.

3.

Bali:

A Glimpse into

Another World

I will be including in this book a lot of material from Bali, because it is the living example of so much of what I teach. The following chapters give precise information on how to create sacred space in your own home, but first let's take a journey into a culture where Feng Shui and Space Clearing are already a complete way of life.

THE SEEN AND THE UNSEEN

For the last twenty years, I have really been living two parallel existences. Part of me is firmly based in the material, seen world, and the other half of me lives in the metaphysical, unseen world of energy and vibration.

One of the reasons I love spending so much time in Bali is that the Balinese all live in these two worlds too. They call them *sekala* (the seen world) and *niskala* (the unseen world), and they understand very well that everything manifest in the physical world has its origin and counterpart in the unseen realms of energy. I feel tremendous empathy with the Balinese people, and their beautiful island is the only place I know where there are three million people living a totally integrated, vibrant, spiritual way of life. Bali is one place in the world where I don't need to explain myself. The people understand exactly what I'm doing in my life.

A   CEREMONIAL   WAY   OF   LIFE

In the West we differentiate between our material and our spiritual lives. Not so in Bali. Their religion pulsates through every aspect of their lives. They have developed a uniquely theatrical form of Hinduism that incorporates animism and ancestor worship. This is no stodgy, serious affair— religion in Bali is immensely good fun, which accounts for the enthusiastic participation of young and old alike.

There is nothing the Balinese like more than a three-day temple ceremony, which is both a religious and a social event. They will spend days beforehand preparing elaborate offerings of food and flowers for the gods, and then, being practical people, several more days consuming the food after the gods have availed themselves of the essence of it! Since each village has three temples, and each temple has a major festival approximately twice a year, there is always a ceremony happening somewhere on Bali. It is estimated that there are more than twenty thousand temples on the island, which is astonishing when you consider that it is no more than fifty miles from north to south and ninety miles from east to west!

The Balinese believe that they live in a paradise on earth, and they honor and respect the land they live on. Every dwelling has its own shrine, and offerings of flowers, incense, and holy water are made to the gods three times every day, at dawn, at midday, and at dusk. They truly live in perfect harmony with their environment.

One of my favorite stories illustrates this relationship perfectly. There are very few things in Bali that can give you a serious bite, but one of these is a centipede that grows up to several inches long. Its bite isn't fatal, but it is incredibly painful. One night I got bitten by one in my home while I was asleep. Its fangs left two bruised puncture holes in two places on my torso, and I was in agony for hours. The next morning all our Balinese neighbors came to ask what all the commotion in the night had been about. We explained what had happened, and they immediately wanted to examine the bites. Having looked at them, off they went.

"Don't I get any sympathy?" I exclaimed to Rai, who was at the time my Balinese husband-to-be. He shook his head, smiled, and gently explained that the Balinese view of why I had been bitten was that I had done something to offend the earth spirits. What our neighbors had gone to do was to put extra offerings on the ground outside their homes so they wouldn't get bitten too! He said that we should do likewise to avert further visitations. We did so and have never been troubled since.

FENG SHUI IN BALI

One reason why Bali is such a paradise island is because the art of Feng Shui is so highly developed there that it is as if the buildings seem to grow out of the very ground itself. They fit so snugly into their surroundings that, for all intents and purposes, it looks as if they have grown from seed and put down roots into the earth. This is why virtually every view looks like such a perfect picture postcard.

Rather than this skill being confined to a few skilled professionals, all Balinese people have a strongly developed natural sense of harmony, which extends to their relationships with each other, their surroundings, and the greater cosmos. I have never met a Balinese person who didn't have a natural aptitude for Feng Shui, and I often marvel at how they can create such immense beauty so effortlessly. They don't raze the vegetation to the ground and build sterile concrete little boxes as we do. They sculpt the dwellings into the natural contours of the land, accentuating and enhancing every detail. They do not arrange things in neat rows or try to make houses look the same. Their homes are an extension of themselves and an expression of their spiritual values and individual creativity.

The Balinese live very close to the land. They like to smell the earth, hear the sounds of nature, be awakened by the sound of cocks crowing, and lulled to sleep by the sounds of crickets or frogs. Even in urban areas, they utilize every element of earth, air, fire, and water to create a deep sense of connection to the place in which they live.

Life in Bali is constantly moving. This is reflected in the fact that there are no past or future tenses in the language—they simply live in the Now. The people have an innate creativity and do not resist change in the way that Western people do. This is one reason why their traditional way of life has survived, because they easily adapt and incorporate new influences arriving from the West into their own culture. One wonderful example of this is a ceremony called *Tumpek Landep*, which is held every 210 days. Traditionally, offerings are made on this day to metal weapons of war. With their warring days over, the Balinese have adapted the ceremony to current times and now take their metal cars, motorbikes, and trucks to the local temple to be blessed! The radiator grills and wing mirrors are all adorned with intricate offerings made from plaited coconut leaves, which flap in the wind until they finally blow away. Offerings are also made to other pieces of "iron" equipment such as computers.

BUILDING A NEW HOUSE IN BALI

Houses in Bali are traditionally built according to the body measurements of the head of the household, to be sure of creating an environment that is totally harmonious for that family. Can you imagine what it must feel like to live in a house that has been designed according to your own personal body measurements?! It must feel incredible, like putting on a comfortable overcoat that has been tailored by experts to a perfect fit.

The process begins by consulting an expert about the most auspicious day to begin planning the new home. The Balinese have two calendars running alongside the Gregorian calendar—the *Saka* lunar calendar and the *Pawukon* 210-day calendar. A fascinating aspect of the *Pawukon* calendar is that the passing years are not numbered. The cycle just repeats itself again and again forever. It contains within it a one-day week, a two-day week, a three-day week, and so on up to a ten-day week. Auspicious days for different activities are determined by when these weeks intersect, the most important generally being the three-, five-, and seven-day weeks. It is the eight-day week that is used to determine matters relating to building.

The traditional principles of architecture in Bali are called *Asta Kosala Kosali*, and a traditional architect is called an *undagi*. While all Balinese people know what "feels" right, if they can afford to, they will employ one of these architects to calculate the exact mathematical proportions and oversee the building construction.

On the first visit by the head of the household to the *undagi*, dozens of measurements will be taken from his body. The length of fingers, feet, arms, and so on are added together and multiplied to determine the size of the entrance gate, the compound walls, the upright posts, and so on. As an example, one unit of measurement is the *depa*, which is the distance between a person's fingertips when his arms are outstretched to either side at shoulder height as far as they will go. Added to these basic measurements is a fascinating extra something called a *urip*, which in the case of the *depa* is the width of the fist. *Urip* literally translates as "something that triggers life," and by adding this extra something, the building becomes more than just the materials it is made of.

In the West we generally build anywhere we please, with no thought for the earth spirits that may inhabit any particular plot of land. In Bali, sites are very carefully selected so that harmony is maintained between the humans and the unseen beings that coexist in the space. If there are resident earth spirits who cannot be coaxed to "relocate," building will not proceed on that site. Another spot will be chosen. There is no question of buildings being erected out of economic necessity in Bali, because no one would dare to live in such a house. Nor would anyone build a house on an impure site such as an ex-burial ground or a place where a great tragedy had taken place.

BUILDING CEREMONIES

A number of different ceremonies are held throughout the building process, commencing with a foundation ceremony. Each Balinese village has its own particular customs, so foundation ceremonies vary enormously in different parts of the island. One version of the ceremony for important buildings and temples is that offerings of five different metals (gold, silver, bronze, copper, and iron) and a yellow coconut with five different colors of thread wrapped around it are placed in the ground. For humbler dwellings, a few bricks simply wrapped in a piece of white cloth are enough. Holy water, flowers, incense, mantras, and prayers for the building work to proceed harmoniously are added to complete either ceremony.

For sacred buildings, wood has to come from a living tree, and offer-

ings must be made to the tree before taking the timber. For general building purposes, the rules are more relaxed, although it is still very important
that timber uprights are positioned in the same direction the wood grew in
as a tree.

Another ceremony is held at the time when the building materials start
being joined together and, when the work is finally complete, an auspicious day is chosen to perform a big consecration ceremony called *pame-
laspasan*. Until this has been done, no one may sleep in the building, no fire
may be lit, and no lights may be turned on.

The purpose of the consecration ceremony is to ensure the safety and
harmony of the inhabitants and also to bring the building to life. No Balinese person would ever want to live or work in a building that was "dead."
The Balinese consider that in the process of building, all the building materials have been killed. The stones have been killed as they were taken
from the earth, the trees have been killed as they were felled, the grasses
have been killed as they were cut, and so on. The cost of this vital consecration ceremony is so substantial that banks are familiar with making pro-
vision for it in the amount of any loan for building work.

MICROCOSMS AND MACROCOSMS

In the Christian Bible, it says, "Man is built in the image of God." The Balinese take this one step further. They build their buildings in the image of
man! On many different levels, they create small microcosms that mirror
the greater macrocosm.

They have a concept known as *Tri Angga*, meaning three components
or parts. The human body is seen to be composed of a head, a torso, and
the legs and feet. The head is considered to be sacred, the middle neutral,
and the legs and feet profane.

In designing a house, the household shrine will be placed in the "head"
position, the general living quarters in the "torso" area, and the animals and
rubbish pits will be located in the "feet" area. Temples are constructed with
three courtyards so that the highest shrines are in the "head," more general
ceremonies take place in the middle, and everyday activities happen in the

outer courtyard. Even whole villages are designed according to the same principle. Each village contains three separate temples, the most sacred being in the "head" position, where the highest ceremonies are held; the middle temple is for more general ceremonies; and the lower temple is called the "temple of the dead" and is adjacent to the local cemetery where bodies are placed awaiting cremation.

ORIENTATION

On an even grander scale, the whole of Bali is seen by the Balinese in terms of these three divisions. The sacred mountains that form a ridge from east to west through the center of the island are high, the middle area between the mountains and the coast is where most of the Balinese live, and the sea is low.

The Balinese Hindus (95 percent of Bali's population) believe that the gods live in these mountains, the tallest and most sacred of which is Mount Agung. All Balinese homes are built so that the most sacred part of the home (the temple) is pointing toward Mount Agung, and all beds are aligned so that the people sleep with their heads pointing toward it too. If for any reason this is impossible, the next most sacred directions are toward another nearer mountain or toward the east.

Anthropologists have been trying for decades to explain Bali's amazing resilience to the ravages of tourism but have never thought to examine this aspect. Anyone who has ever done a group meditation where everyone lies down with their heads to the center knows how powerful it can be. It is as if something extra comes to join the group, over and above the sum total of the individuals present. The effect of the Balinese people aligning themselves to their religious purpose every night of their lives in this way is immense. No matter how many tourists come and go, this practice continues. Every night as they sleep, they reinforce their joint spiritual purpose and their incredible community spirit. They are creating sacred space on a national scale!

Balinese people become physically disoriented if they don't sleep aligned in this way. It is as if their bodies become magnetized to the vol-

Mount Agung

The island of Bali

canoes. In fact it is said that you can take Balinese people, blindfold them, spin them around, and then ask them which way the mountains are, and they will be able to tell you. I had great fun testing this theory on some willing volunteers and was impressed by their accuracy!

If you go to Bali hoping to experience this, you will find that some tourist accommodations are built according to these principles, but the Balinese have long since realized that tourists don't care a bit about it, so they are increasingly building hotels with no regard for placement of beds. From time to time, I leave my home in Bali and go traveling around the island, and if I take a room where the bed needs moving, there are always delighted smiles that I know and care about such things and many willing hands to help me move it.

OTHER FORMS OF CONSECRATION IN BALI

The Balinese consecrate not only buildings but also cars, musical instruments, and sacred objects such as dance masks and priests' bells. Having made consecrations, offerings are then made on a regular basis to keep the energy vibration high. I always joke that my car in Bali needs three things to keep it going: gas in the gas tank, water in the radiator, and flowers on the dashboard!

SPACE CLEARING IN BALI

What happens in Bali is that they Space Clear the whole island on a daily basis, which means that low level energies are swept away (see the following chapter). This is another reason why, in spite of the huge increase in tourism, the spiritual culture has stayed intact. Even to this day, rape and incest are virtually unheard of on the island. Theft, too, used to be extremely rare but has been on the increase since the onset of the major economic crisis of 1998. The villages are still pretty safe but visitors need to be cautious in any densely populated areas. Bali is also one island (perhaps the only one?) in the world where none of the women work as prostitutes. They simply will not do it. There are prostitutes on the island, but they come from other Indonesian islands, never from Bali itself. You really could call Bali the purification center of the planet.

"NYEPI"

No description of Bali would be complete without including its extraordinary annual Space Clearing ceremony called *Nyepi*, which takes place each March and marks the beginning of the Balinese New Year. In the weeks leading up to this day, children are allowed to set off firecrackers all over the place to frighten away evil spirits, and in many parts of the island giant papier mâché demons called *ogoh-ogoh* are created in each of the villages. On the night before *Nyepi*, they have fabulous parades of these demons carried through the streets on bamboo frames by the young men of the villages and accompanied by crashing cymbals and mobile, xylophone-like gamelan orchestras playing at full volume. The idea is to make as much noise as possible, and it is an unforgettable audiovisual experience.

At midnight, the *ogoh-ogoh* effigies are set down at crossroads throughout the island, together with copious offerings to the *bhuta kala* (low or angry spirits) they represent. After a grand ceremony, the *ogoh-ogoh* are set on fire. The Balinese understand that crossroads are intersections for energy as well as traffic, and they believe that the reason accidents so commonly happen at crossroads is because of the angry spirits that congregate there. By making these offerings and setting fire to the effigies, their intention is to placate the spirits and purify these places. Many people stay up throughout the night making as much noise as possible until dawn, when stillness reigns throughout the land.

Nyepi day in Bali is incredible. It is the only place on earth where for one day of the year everything comes to a complete standstill throughout the land. No one is allowed to go out on the roads, either on foot or by transport. Until recently no planes were allowed to land, but this caused such havoc with international airline schedules that the Balinese government has now conceded that planes may land, but new arrivals are escorted by police directly to hotels, where they must stay put for the rest of the day. Apart from a few essential services, no one is allowed to work. No equipment may be operated or lights turned on. No fires may be lit, so no one may cook (the Balinese have devised ingenious ways of keeping cooked food fresh overnight without refrigeration). There is no playing of music, no watching television, no listening to the radio (all the local stations are closed for the day in any case), and no using the telephone. In some areas of Bali, the electricity supplies are actually turned off for twenty-four hours to enforce the law. Smoking, gambling, and drinking alcohol are not allowed, and talking is only in hushed tones. Even the dogs stop barking, and the chickens stop clucking! The lush tropical silence envelops you like a warm, sweet dream.

For one whole day, there is nowhere you have to be and nothing you have to do. What happens is that all your internal organs come to rest and c-o-m-p-l-e-t-e-ly r-e-l-a-x. It is the most amazing experience. It is a time for meditating and dwelling on your life and for focusing on what you want to happen in the following year. After nightfall, the effect is even more profound as you sit surrounded by complete darkness and complete silence in the mellow companionship of those you love, mulling over the previous year and contemplating the new. It feels like it could go on for ever, and you wish it would.

The next day, everything is back to normal. With the first rays of dawn, the roads fill with people, bikes, cars, trucks, and buses, and *Nyepi* feels like it really was a dream . . . until next year.

SACRED TEACHINGS OF BALI

The Balinese may not have the material possessions that we have in the West, but they have a richness of spirit that shines out of them. There is much we can learn from their remarkable culture, and I will be showing you in this book how some of their wisdoms and practices can be integrated into our Western way of life to enhance the quality of our own lives. In particular, the Space Clearing techniques in the following chapters incorporate wonderfully effective elements of Balinese ceremonies, which I have adapted for use in the West. The next chapter explains how it all works.

4.

What Is Space Clearing?

Space Clearing is the art of cleansing and consecrating spaces. To understand why this practice is so important, it is first of all necessary to understand how we, as humans, process energy.

THE ASTRAL LIGHT

The atmosphere of the planet contains not just the air that we breathe but also invisible energy called astral light, of which there are seven levels ranging from the very low (which is not in itself "bad" but in modern times has become very psychically polluted) to the very high and spiritually refined. We have the possibility of breathing in and processing any one of these seven levels at any time, although most people are unaware of this and generally live their lives at the lower levels. Certain places on the planet naturally host very high levels of the astral light, and the ancients, who were entirely conscious of this fact, sited temples and sacred structures in those places to enable people to access the higher levels more easily (if you notice, when you visit these sacred sites, your breathing involuntarily becomes very shallow if you are unaccustomed to processing such levels).

To give another example of the effects of these different levels of the astral light, have you ever had the experience of having a sudden flash of understanding about something and then, several hours later, not being able to remember your insight at all? This is because flashes of understanding exist at a higher level of the astral light than ordinary everyday life. The only way to reconnect with the understanding is to reconnect with the level you were at when it happened.

WHY SPACE CLEARING IS NECESSARY

Every religion in the world offers its devotees ceremonies or rituals to elevate them temporarily to levels of the astral light they cannot easily attain by themselves so that they can experience enhanced states of being. To facilitate this, temples are constantly purified to maintain their atmospheres at high levels, especially at times of high ceremonies.

All Space Clearing is designed to raise the level of the astral light of atmospheres in our own personal spaces and, in so doing, raise the quality of life that it is possible for us to experience. In other words, depending on your knowledge and skill, you can use these techniques to cleanse the astral light and create sacred space wherever you are. If you want your life to be more meaningful and purposeful than the general level it is being lived at today by so many people, learning how to purify your atmospheres will be of great benefit.

ENERGY IN BUILDINGS

Energetically, everything that ever happens in a building goes out in ripples, like the effect of a stone being dropped in a pond, and is recorded in the walls, the floor, the ceiling, the furniture, objects, plants, animals, and people in that space. It gets imprinted in the very fabric of the structure. Repetitive patterns get deeply imprinted, as do moods and atmospheres. Any events accompanied by strong emotions or trauma are recorded more intensely. If you have ever had the experience of walking into a room after there has just been an argument, you know that you can literally feel it hanging in the air. People sometimes say, "You could have cut the tension with a knife!," meaning that the tension in the air was so dense, it was as if the argument were physically tangible.

The residue of these energy ripples accumulates around the edges of the room and builds up, particularly in corners, nooks, and crannies.

It is an interesting fact that some native cultures will not live in buildings with corners. The Zulus and the Native Americans, for example, live in round buildings. They say that "evil" dwells in corners, and mostly what they are describing is the way low level energy sticks in those areas.

In our Western culture, children are usually more sensitive to this than adults. They will tell you they don't like spooky corners, spaces under beds, or sleeping with closet doors open. This is a perfectly natural human response, even for grown-ups!

If you are reading this book inside a building, stop for a minute, look up from the book, and imagine what the place you are in would look like if it had never physically been cleaned since the time it was built. Imagine the buildup of dust, cobwebs, and so on. The worst areas would be in the corners, nooks, and crannies. Well, of course no one would ever want to live or work in such a space, but on an energetic level, that is exactly how a building looks and feels if it has never been Space Cleared. Hot, sticky, electrical cobwebs and congealed clumps of static energy accumulate in all the corners, nooks, and crannies.

Everyone creates a certain amount of psychic debris on a daily basis, which leaves a residue in the astral light of their homes in the same way as everyday living creates a need for cleaning and tidying to be done on a physical level. As Jane Alexander so succinctly put it in her article about Space Clearing in the *Daily Mail* in 1994, "Most of us are probably living in the psychic equivalent of a garbage dump."

Very few Western homes are so well designed that there are no areas where energy gets stuck. Most buildings are designed without any thought being given to the way energy can flow around them, and awkwardly positioned furniture can then add to the problems. How much stuck energy builds up depends on the Feng Shui of a place (how well energy flows around it) and the activities of the people who are living in the place.

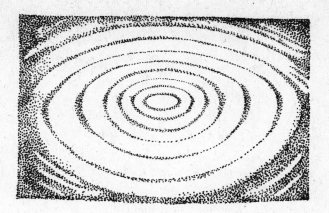

Energy ripples outward and accumulates, especially in corners

I have Space Cleared ancestral homes centuries old where the buildup of stuck energy stood three feet thick off the walls and felt like psychic molasses. I have also Space Cleared twenty-year-old buildings that felt nearly as dense, simply due to the amount of mental and emotional traffic in that space in such a short period of time.

ENERGY IN OBJECTS

Objects can be Space Cleared too. All objects become impregnated with the energy of what happens around them. If you buy something second-hand, it will carry the energy traces of the person who owned it before. If it was used a lot, used for a long time, or had very strong emotional connections for that person, the emanations will be correspondingly stronger.

This is the whole basis of psychometry, that a trained person can hold, say, a ring belonging to another person, and can translate the vibrational frequency of that ring and describe everything about the person without ever meeting him or her. And this is also why so many people want to have something that belonged to or was touched by a holy person or a saint. It is why personal belongings of movie stars, football heroes, and the like are so sought after. People want to own something that has the energy imprint of the owner on it. An autograph combines the energy flow from the hand of the famous person with an illustration of that person's energy matrix, which anyone skilled in the art of reading handwriting will soon be able to decipher. It is the next best thing to having something that belonged to the person.

U SES OF S PACE C LEARING

To enhance Feng Shui placement

Space Clearing works beautifully in conjunction with traditional Chinese Feng Shui placement. It makes any Feng Shui enhancements work much more easily, smoothly, and deeply. The two naturally go hand in hand. Space Clearing also allows you to experience the energy of your space much more intimately, so Feng Shui changes naturally suggest themselves to you.

    If I am booked to do a combined Space Clearing and Feng Shui consultation, I will usually Space Clear first, go around and sense the energy again, and then look at Feng Shui placement. To have Space Clearing and Feng Shui placement done at the same time is a very powerful and transformational experience, which can be a real turning point in a person's life. This is why I have included information about both subjects in this book.

Clearing stuckness in your life

Many people decide to learn Space Clearing because they feel stuck in some problem or other. Whenever you feel stuck in some issue in your life, there is always a corresponding stuckness in some part of your home and, by clearing the energy in your home and getting it moving again, the problem starts to resolve.

    One woman I know had been trying to find a new house to rent, and after several weeks of trying she was despairing. She was willing to pay a good price for something nice in the right area, but every time she found a house that fit the bill, it was rented to someone else before she was able to clinch the deal. The situation was getting urgent because the lease on her present home had nearly expired. She didn't think it would do much good, but she decided to Space Clear her house anyway. Within twenty-four hours she had signed a new lease for a place that was everything she had wanted. She told me, "It was as if somebody let out the cork, and a whole river of success flowed into my life!"

Another woman who had her own business told me, "I had a big decision to make and just couldn't decide what to do. Then I remembered your advice and started cleaning, straightening up, and Space Clearing my home. As I did so, I distinctly felt my inner confusion dissolve. By the time I had finished I was so clear about what I wanted to do that I could hardly wait to begin!"

A couple told me they had been wanting to buy the apartment they lived in for the last eight years, but the owner had refused to sell it. After Space Clearing the apartment, the owner contacted them the next day and said he was willing to sell!

Something that I love about Space Clearing is that the basics of it can be taught very easily, which means that you can learn it and then take personal responsibility for clearing your own stuckness when you need to.

Clearing recurring problems

Another situation where Space Clearing is useful is if you keep having the same problems again and again. Maybe it is the same argument that keeps coming up with your family or your partner and never gets resolved. Space Clearing will not remove the cause of the argument, but it will give you a fresh start so that you are more likely to resolve it once and for all.

One very moving story concerns a woman whose daughter had broken off communications with her for many years. While I was Space Clearing her apartment, the daughter called to talk to her and to arrange to meet up. They now enjoy a close mother-and-daughter relationship again.

Another woman was married to a man who was prone to going off and sulking for weeks on end if he didn't get his own way. This had been going on for years, and she was really fed up with it. The next time it happened, she Space Cleared the house, paying particular attention to the Relationships area (see Chapter 18 about the bagua to discover where this area is in your own home). A few hours later, for the first time ever, he phoned to apologize and came home to talk the problem through. A year later she called to tell me, "He hasn't stormed off in a huff ever since. We sit and discuss our problems now like reasonable people. There's no doubt in my mind that Space Clearing saved my marriage."

Clearing predecessor energy

Predecessor energy is about how history tends to repeat itself. Maybe it's not your own stuck energy but the psychic residue of people who have lived in the space before you that is affecting your life. If, for example, the last people who lived in your home got divorced, the chances are extremely high that the people who lived there before them also got divorced or separated, and the chances are that you will also have similar relationship difficulties, simply because that energy is still hanging around. If you move into a new home and notice after a while that you are all putting on weight, check to see if the previous occupants were fat people. If you start sleeping a lot, it may well be that the last tenants used to sleep a lot. Predecessor energy can affect you in many ways that you would never think of unless you know how to read the energy of what has happened in the space before you arrived.

Space Clearing is a very effective way of clearing this energy out to leave you with a completely fresh start. It is always best to Space Clear and consecrate anywhere you live, ideally before you move in, and I will be showing you exactly how to do this.

For healing

One of the first things that happens if you are admitted to a hospital in Russia is that you are given an enema. This is because the medical profession there understands that the body's natural ability to heal itself is greatly enhanced if the eliminatory channels are clear. This can be taken one stage further by Space Clearing the psychic discharge that occurs during the healing process and accumulates in the sickroom.

Space Clearing promotes healing on a physical level and also aids emotional healing where there is depression, grief, and so on. I have received many letters and phone calls from people letting me know that it has helped them with a whole range of health problems, from minor to chronic ailments.

One couple told me, "At 6 P.M. we were both sneezing, a bit feverish, had sore throats, and knew we were coming down with the flu. We Space Cleared the apartment, went straight to bed, slept like babies, and woke up the next morning absolutely fine!"

Another man told me, "I had been depressed for years, and nothing had helped. A friend came and helped me Space Clear my home, and the energy lift it gave me was incredible. Now I'm back at work again and am enjoying my life. I just have to remember to Space Clear at the first sign of depression setting in, before it gets a grip on me."

Pay particular attention to item 3 of the preparation for Space Clearing checklist in Chapter 6 if you or anyone in the space you want to clear is ill.

After an illness

Always wash the bedding, clean the sickroom, and Space Clear your entire home after there has been an illness to clear out the energy and refresh the space.

It is my fondest hope that one day teams of Space Clearers will go regularly into the hospitals of the world. Can you imagine how much discharged energy must build up in a hospital ward where people are constantly sick or dying? Can you imagine how much that stacks the odds against your getting well in that space? You are already weak and vulnerable when you arrive there and probably fearful of what may happen. Every fear you have is an open invitation for a wandering thoughtform to march on in, so then you take on board all the psychic debris of all the people who have been sick in that space before you as well as your own.

At the moment I am in the process of developing techniques whereby

Space Clearing can be done without having to move sick people out of the room. One stumbling block is that it is almost always necessary to Space Clear the bed too, which of course is difficult to do if someone is lying in it! However, more and more doctors and nurses are now taking my workshop, and some have started Space Clearing private hospital rooms after one patient leaves and before the next one arrives, and even wards where it is possible to take all the patients out while they are doing it. They are reporting back wonderful results.

After there has been a death in a place

If you sell a house in the state of Washington, you must indicate in the deed of sale whether someone has committed suicide in it. In certain Native American traditions, a home cannot be lived in again if someone has died in it. Many people from many different cultures have very uneasy feelings about living in a place where there has been a death.

The problem is usually not the dying, unless it was a violent death. Dying is a perfectly natural process. It is the transition from this physical world back into the energetic realms, and learning how to die well is a great art. The problem is usually the grief and emotion that lingers in a place after a death, and Space Clearing is a very effective way of clearing this so that life can carry on.

Manifesting what you want in your life

Space Clearing creates room for expansion. You can use it to expand your creativity, prosperity, a particular skill, or anything you want to do. It helps you manifest what you want in your life more easily, because by clearing the energy field in your home, your personal energy field (aura) is clearer, so the messages that you send out to the universe are clearer and more easily received. You create a space in which something new can happen, and the universe (which abhors a vacuum) can happily fill it with what you want.

One man, previously a total skeptic, told me, "The week after I Space Cleared my home, I started a new relationship and was offered a contract in Singapore, all expenses paid." Many people confirm that magical things start happening in their lives after they start Space Clearing.

To enhance your spiritual development

We live in a time of great change. As we approach the end of the millennium, new developments are happening faster and faster. The clearer and more flexible you are, the more easily you will be able to adapt to and move with the times. Space Clearing clears out the past so that you can be fully present in the now and keeps the energy field of your home sparkling clean and clear to give you the best environment for personal growth. I personally use Space Clearing more for this purpose and for manifesting change in my life than for anything else these days.

For increased vitality

Space Clearing is a great remedy for couch-potato syndrome, tiredness, and fatigue. It is also helpful for convalescents and people with myalgic encephalomyelitis.

It works because revitalizing the atmospheres in your home has a corresponding effect in your own energy field. Pay particular attention to any room in which you habitually feel more tired than usual and use Space Clearing in your bedroom for improved quality of sleep. Also check that you are not draining your energy by exposing yourself to electromagnetic fields for long periods of time (see Chapters 14 and 15), and clear out any clutter you have accumulated.

To improve your sex life!

Sex is about exchanging energies between two people, so it is obviously enhancing to a relationship to have sex in a space that is as energetically clear as possible. This is particularly important if you are starting a new relationship in a place where you previously had another lover! You can use Space Clearing to clear out your old relationship and keep the passion in the new!

To make a place feel really special

If you have a room in your house you would like to use as a sanctuary for meditation, prayer, healing, or something similar, begin by Space Clearing it and then set the atmospheres you want. Space Clearing makes a place look and feel brighter and clearer, as if the energy is twinkling!

To change an atmosphere

Sometimes you may want to do Space Clearing just to change the way a place feels. This may be after an argument or after someone has been to stay for a while, to clear out their frequencies and reintroduce your own; it may be to reinstate normality after a party that has left the place feeling worse for wear or just simply to give your atmospheres a perk to cheer yourself up.

To give you a sense of belonging in a place

Something that people often say to me after Space Clearing their homes is that they feel more "at home" afterward, and safer. In some cases, people have lived in a place for ten years or more and never felt that they put down roots at all until they did Space Clearing.

For travelers

You can use Space Clearing to transform any hotel room that you stay in. By knowing how to clear out the stale energy of previous occupants, you can create a feeling of being at home wherever you go and will enjoy much better quality of sleep.

For therapists

I worked for many years as a therapist, and I came to realize that no therapist can heal another person. People can only heal themselves. But what a therapist can do is create a very safe space for people to do their own healing in, channel universal energy for their benefit, and use their particular skills and talents to support them through their healing process.

Something I noticed during my time as a therapist was that all my colleagues periodically went through bouts of therapists' "burn out," and I never did. I guessed (correctly, I now know) that Space Clearing was the magic ingredient that was making the difference. If you work as a therapist, Space Clearing your therapy room regularly creates a sacred place for your clients to feel really safe and let go on a very deep level. This produces much better results for them and also means that you don't get "burned out" yourself because you're not taking their "stuff" on board personally.

If you are doing healing or therapy work at home, it is even more important to Space Clear regularly. It is best to have a separate room you use only for your healing work and to use separate bedding materials, towels, and so on. Certainly never sleep in the same space your clients occupy when you are working with them.

Health clinics and alternative healing centers also need regular Space Clearing to clear out the energies discharged during healing. This benefits the clients and also the practitioners.

For workshop leaders

The only place I have ever taught a workshop that didn't need Space Clearing before I began was at Alternatives in St. James's Church, Piccadilly, London. The natural harmonious flow of energy in the building and the history of high-quality workshops and events happening in the space was so unique that I didn't need to. Elsewhere I always turn up an hour or so earlier than I would otherwise need to so that I can Space Clear before I begin.

I know other workshop leaders who now swear by it too. Once they have tried Space Clearing they never want to teach without it again, because it makes it so much easier for them and for the participants. The atmosphere is lighter, the energy flows better, the participants stay focused, they get the information more clearly, and everyone leaves feeling energized.

To improve harmony and productivity in the office

Space Clearing helps to produce more harmony in the workplace, which leads to better productivity. After one business owner started Space Clearing regularly, he said, "People come in and say the atmosphere feels much clearer and happier. I think Space Clearing makes a tremendous difference. We all enjoy coming to work much more these days."

Some businesses like to use Space Clearing before important meetings such as board meetings. They feel it helps the meeting to arrive at the best possible decision for everyone concerned with the minimum of wrangles.

Regular Space Clearing also helps to reduce levels of electromagnetic pollution generated by computers and other office equipment.

To enhance profits in business

Use Space Clearing if sales ever start to drop. Freshening and revitalizing the space has a corresponding effect on the business.

The first time I taught this workshop in Sydney, Australia, I got an excited call two days later from one of the participants who was a shopowner. She told me, "I tried Space Clearing my shop straight after the workshop on Sunday. I rarely sell anything on Mondays, but by 4 P.M. I had doubled my usual takings, and by 5 P.M. they had tripled!"

Of course not everyone experiences such miraculous results, but most people do experience substantial improvements. One company in London used Space Clearing because business was slow and called me a month later to ask how to stop the phone calls coming in so thick and fast because they couldn't keep up with demand. Some businesses now contract me on a regular basis to Space Clear their premises several times a year.

For "luck"

When things are going right, it feels like you are surfing on the crest of a wave, and you just get carried along by it. I don't believe in "good" or "bad" luck as such. I believe we create our own reality. But what can happen is that you get off the track or fall off the wave, and at these times nothing seems to go right. Space Clearing gives you a fresh start and helps you climb back on top of the wave so that you start to move with the universal flow of energy again.

This list of uses to which Space Clearing can be put is constantly expanding, so these are by no means the only applications. I am discovering new ones all the time.

In the next chapter the first steps of Space Clearing are explained, which are to do with clearing clutter. This is always one of the most popular sections when I teach this material as a workshop, and the information is absolutely vital to Space Clearing, traditional Feng Shui, and any kind of personal work to manifest positive changes in your life.

5.

Clearing Clutter

The whole art of Space Clearing begins with clearing out any clutter you have accumulated, straighten your place up, and giving it a good spring cleaning. The more thoroughly you do this, the better the results you will get from the rest of the information in this book.

CLUTTER IS STUCK ENERGY

Never underestimate the effect of clutter on your life. Whenever I meet people who tell me they are stuck, I know that if I visit their homes I will almost always find lots of clutter. Clutter accumulates when energy stagnates.

Healthy energy is moving energy. Think what happens when a pool of water stagnates. Very soon it becomes murky and starts to smell. This is similar to what happens energetically when people live surrounded by clutter. In the early years when I started this work, I developed not only my ability to sense atmospheres but also my senses of smell, hearing, and so on. I can literally smell clutter when I walk into someone's house, even if it is hidden away from sight in closets and under beds. It has a certain musty, pervasive kind of odor.

Most people who have lots of clutter say they can't find the energy to begin to clear it. They constantly feel tired. This is because everything you own is connected to you by strands of energy. When you live surrounded by clutter it is like dragging the ball and chain of your past around with you everywhere you go. No wonder you feel tired.

Clearing clutter actually releases huge amounts of energy in the body. When you get rid of everything in your life that has no real meaning or significance for you, you literally feel lighter in body, mind, and spirit. When everything you have around you is sacred to you, your whole life becomes sacred. You can live in present time and move with the flow. This explains why the cultures with few material possessions are often the most spiritually intact, whereas cultures that own lots of things often lose their spiritual focus completely.

People unconsciously keep clutter in order to suppress their own aliveness. They may want to change and improve their lives, but their subconscious minds are afraid to journey into the unknown. If you have lots of clutter, understand that you have it because on some level you need it right now. Understanding why you need it helps you to begin to release your clutter and cease to accumulate it in the future.

Twice in my life I have gotten rid of everything I owned and started again. Both times it was an incredibly scary yet incredibly refreshing, regenerative experience, a real turning point in my life. One English woman who came to one of my workshops got so inspired that she went home and cleared out all but five items of clothing from her closet. She got rid of her ancient stereo system and stacks and stacks of junk. In doing this, she released huge amounts of stuck energy, which created space for something new to come in. A week later she received a check in the mail from her mother for seven thousand dollars, and she went straight out and bought herself a whole new wardrobe of wonderful clothes, a new sound system, and everything else she wanted. She told me the check was totally unexpected and that the last time her mother had sent her any money was ten years earlier! I don't recommend that everyone does this, but it certainly worked for her.

Another woman wrote and told me, "You left me at 2 P.M., I had had no lunch, yet I worked till midnight on your suggestions for the apartment. I have now implemented all your Feng Shui ideas. I was full of energy and

Clutter!

somehow had been released to clear so much clutter that had previously resisted my best endeavors."

Denise Linn once told a wonderful story in one of her seminars about the time when she used to work as a one-on-one therapist. It happened that a client called her up and said he was on the verge of committing suicide. At that precise moment, she was at a crucial point in a session with another client, and so she told the young man, kindly but firmly, "Listen, I can't talk to you right now. Go and clear out two drawers and call me back in an hour." I can just imagine his reaction. He probably thought Denise either hadn't quite heard him or hadn't understood the gravity of the situation. But in fact she had heard and had understood, and when he called back an hour later after clearing out the drawers, the crisis had passed and he was well on his way to finding his own solution to the problem that had overwhelmed him earlier.

There is something immensely therapeutic about clearing your clutter. The reason is that while you are clearing things on an external level, there is a corresponding change going on internally too. What's outside is always inside, and vice versa. Being clear of clutter is one of the greatest aids I know to manifesting the life you want, and it is absolutely essential if you truly want to know joy and happiness in your life. When you experience joy, it is a feeling of great energy flowing through your body, and this cannot happen if your channels are clogged.

The time when most people's clutter surfaces is when they move, and one reason why moving feels like such hard work is that in the process of packing you sort through all your things and decide what you want to take with you and what you don't. You have to deal with all the mental and emotional connections to each object, which can be exhausting. My general rule of thumb is that if I were moving tomorrow and I would end up with more than one or two garbage bags of stuff to throw away, I've got some sorting out to do right now.

When people book Feng Shui consultations with me, they are asking me to come and suggest changes they can make to their homes to improve the flow of positive energy into their lives. It often turns out that the most valuable advice I can give is to go around with them first of all and tell them frankly, "Get rid of this" and "Get rid of that." Until the clutter is cleared, the effect of any Feng Shui adjustments will be minimal, and they will not get full value from the consultation. Worse still, if they go ahead and implement Feng Shui enhancements such as mirrors or crystals before clearing the clutter, it can actually double their problems.

One woman came to one of my workshops and asked me to come and Space Clear her home. She deliberately set the appointment for several weeks' time so that she would be able to sort through her clutter and throw it out before I came. She did the job so thoroughly and with so much care and attention that when I got there I found I had hardly any Space Clearing work to do. Clearing clutter really perks a place up, and this house was smiling ear to ear!

Other people feel so immobilized by their clutter that if they waited until they had cleared it to have a Feng Shui consultation, they would wait forever. These people really benefit from having a professional point out to them the effect the clutter is having on them, so they become motivated to do something about it.

Keeping things "just in case"

Sometimes people get confused about what actually constitutes clutter. My definition of clutter is things you are keeping that stagnate your energy because they serve no purpose in your life. Often people keep things "just in case," which really means "just in case I can never afford to get one again" or something of the kind.

All those things you are keeping "just in case"—you are telling your subconscious mind to prepare for a situation of neediness in the future, and it will go ahead of you and helpfully create that so that you can say, "I *knew* it would come in handy sooner or later!" If you have lots of things you are keeping because you think like this, you are sending out a message to the universe that you don't trust it to provide for you, and you will always feel vulnerable and insecure about the future.

Being neat

Some people think that because I am such a strong advocate of clearing clutter I must be an obsessively neat person living some minimalist Zen type of existence. Anyone who has ever lived with me would roll on the floor laughing at this idea! My astrological sign is Cancer so I am a natural-born hoarder if ever there was one. It's just that I have discovered that keeping myself clear of clutter makes my life work so much better, so I have learned how to do it.

Having clutter is different from being messy. If I am working on a project, I fill the whole room with it—papers and bits of stuff everywhere. Then I will put it all away and start fresh the next day. Find what works best for you. For me there is something very sterile about being too neat all the time. It doesn't stimulate my creativity at all. Being disorganized or having clutter around me, however, blocks my creativity completely. As soon as I have finished using something, I put it back where it belongs. This creates the space for the next thing to happen.

Spring cleaning your home

Remember the old saying, "Cleanliness is next to godliness"? This whole book is about how things work on an energy level, and the simple fact is that if your home is dirty, the energy field around your body (your aura) will be dirty too. And if you clean your home but never bother to clean those awkward bits—under beds, on top of cupboards, behind closets, inside bathroom cabinets, and so on—then there will always be dull, stagnating areas in your energy field too. Festering food in your refrigerator and greasy "yuck" around your stove are two other prime areas to watch out for.

As an exercise one day, decide to really thoroughly clean something that you normally give only a superficial polish. A good example is a television, a computer, or a cassette player. All of these pieces of equipment usually have icky bits where dust and dirt accumulate. Get yourself an old toothbrush, a clean cloth, and some appropriate cleaning fluid (you can buy it in computer supply shops) and get in there. Do it as a kind of meditation. Do it with love. Do it not as a chore but because this object is a part of your life and you wish to honor yourself. You will be amazed at how good it feels.

Before childbirth, many women have a great urge to clean their homes, to prepare and purify the space for their new child. This is a natural, instinctive reaction. Traditionally Western people give themselves an energy lift by spring cleaning their homes once a year. Imagine what vitality you can have if you keep your home like this all the time! If you don't have the time or the inclination to do this, you don't necessarily have to do it yourself. There are people in this world who love cleaning! Trade your skills with a friend, or pay someone to come and do it for you.

You will get tremendous results if you thoroughly spring clean your home the first time you do Space Clearing and then keep it at that standard from then on.

What to do with unwanted presents

Get rid of them. The very thought of this is horrifying to some people. "But what about when Aunt Jane comes to visit and that expensive object she gave us isn't on the mantelpiece?" Whose mantelpiece is it anyway? Whose life is it anyway? If you love the object, fine, but if you keep it in your home out of fear or obligation, you are giving your power away. Every time you walk into the room and see that object, your energy levels drop. Surround yourself with things you love, which inspire and uplift you. And don't think that "out-of-sight, out-of-mind" will work. You can't keep that object in the closet and just bring it out when Aunt Jane is due to visit. Your subconscious mind still knows you have it on the premises. If you have enough of these unwanted presents around you, your energy network looks like a sieve, with vitality running out all over the place.

Try adopting a whole different philosophy about presents. When you give a present, give it with love and let it go. Allow the recipient complete freedom to do whatever he or she wants with the present. If the thing the person can do most usefully is put it straight in the garbage, fine. If the recipient gives it to someone else, fine (you wouldn't want the person to clutter up his or her space with unwanted presents, would you?). Give others this freedom and you will begin to experience more freedom in your own life too.

C LUTTER ZONES IN YOUR HOME

Where does clutter tend to collect in your home? A cluttered basement corresponds to a cluttered subconscious mind and issues not dealt with. Clutter in your attic can limit your higher aspirations and possibilities. There is no place you can put clutter where it will not affect you. Even if you take it out of the house and stash it in a toolshed, or put it in storage somewhere else, it is still there and still having an effect on your life. The one and only thing you can do with clutter is take responsibility for it and clear it.

Junk rooms

Later in this book there is a section on the Feng Shui bagua (see Chapter 18). This is a grid that reveals which areas of your home relate to which aspects of your life. So, for example, there is an area that is assigned to relationships, one to career, another to prosperity, and so on. If you have a junk room in your home, that corresponding area of your life will be affected.

One of my clients had a conservatory in the Fortunate Blessings area of her home, which was filled with all kinds of junk. She was an excellent therapist but wasn't earning enough money to support herself. After clearing her conservatory and filling it with healthy plants, her income substantially increased.

Another client had accumulated junk in her Relationships area, and all the men she attracted in her life were burdened down with problems. She cleared the area and finally found a man she could build a long-term relationship with.

If there is an area of your life that is not working, check that that area in your home isn't full of clutter!

Your front entrance

Keep this area completely clear. The front entrance to your home represents your approach to the world as you look out, and your approach to your own life as you look in.

If the first thing you see when you walk into your home is clutter or junk, your energy levels will drop before you have even crossed the threshold. Some people like to hang all their coats and put all their shoes in a tiny space just inside the front door. Definitely not a good idea. Others like to put things near the front entrance to remind them to take them out, then end up having to step over the objects again and again. You just create struggle for yourself like this.

A surprising number of environmentally conscious folk use the front entrance area as a place to put the old newspapers, magazines, cans, and plastic bottles they are going to recycle. By placing these items in such a prominent position, you are making a statement (however unconscious it may be) that your approach to life is a constant recycling of the past. This will include ideas, problems, illnesses, relationships, and so on. It will mean that you never learn the lesson the first time round. Recycling is fine, but it is not the best thing for you to set eyes on when you arrive home.

Behind doors

Doors that do not open fully restrict the flow of energy in your life. I have been into homes where there is so much clutter behind doors that there is just a narrow gap for people to squeeze through. Move anything that prevents doors from opening fully, and this includes clothes hanging from hooks behind doors.

Passageways

These are the arteries of your home. Junk in hallways and corridors obstructs the flow of life-bringing energy and places obstacles in your path, so your life lumbers rather than jaunts on its way. Keep all passageways clear of clutter.

Floor level

If you must keep clutter, at least get it off the ground. Many people who suffer depression have lots of clutter at floor level, which constantly pulls their energy down.

Under beds

Piles of junk under your bed will definitely influence the quality of your sleep. If you have one of those beds that has drawers in it, the best thing you can keep in there is clean bed linen. For really high-quality sleep, have nothing in your bedroom except your bed itself!

On top of closets

Clutter stashed on top of closets is like problems hanging over you waiting to be dealt with. It impedes your ability to think clearly and freshly. If you cram things on top of closets in your bedroom, it will affect the quality of your sleep, and if that's the first thing you see when you wake up in the morning, you will tend to wake up sluggishly. If you have lots of clutter stashed in your home higher than eye level, it will have a generally oppressive effect, and you may suffer from headaches.

Clear out your closet

Do you have clothes that you no longer wear but you are keeping "just in case"? One woman shared in one of my workshops that when her husband lost his job, they decided to go out and buy her two really good suits of clothes "just in case" they never had enough money again to buy anything like that. That had been two years ago, and she had never worn either suit. She realized they had wasted their money.

Some people keep things they haven't worn in over twenty years. They say that if they keep them long enough they will come back into style. My advice is, if you haven't worn it in the last year, and especially if you haven't worn it in the last two or three years, then toss it, sell it, exchange it, burn it, or give it away. In one year you will have gone through a cycle of all the seasons, and if you haven't felt the urge to wear it in all that time, then that particular article of clothing has had its time. If two or three cycles of the seasons have gone by without your wearing it, then it is definitely time to let it go.

It may be useful if you can understand why those clothes will never be appropriate again. In the same way that we decorate the walls of our homes, we choose colors, textures, and designs of fabrics that we wear to reflect our own energy vibrations. As an example, people go through color phases. Several years ago my entire wardrobe was purple with a few green, blue, and turquoise items, but it was purple I was really big on. Someone came to find me in Bali and knew which house was mine by the sheer quantity of purple laundry hanging out to dry! At that time I was stacking lots of purple energy into my aura, which was to do with reclaiming my own power and prosperity. Now I have integrated the color, and so I hardly ever wear it.

Most people have some items in their wardrobes that they bought, wore once, and have never worn again. What happens is that you are out shopping one day and your eye catches something, let's say it's orange with purple polka dots. You try it on and it looks fantastic (to you), so you buy it. Well, it so happened that on that particular day you were a bit off balance emotionally and the colors in your aura had changed to orange with purple splotchy bits, or something complementary to those colors, so the new clothes looked great. But by the next day that particular emotional set has dissipated, your aura is back to its usual colors, and the clothes don't look so great to you anymore (they never did to anyone else!). You wait for the cycle to come around again, but usually (mercifully) it's a once-only situation with no repeats. The trick is never go shopping when you feel emotionally out-of-sorts. Comfort shopping is one sure way to end up with a wardrobe of clothes you will never wear.

Some people keep clothes that are too small for them because they are planning to lose weight so that they can wear them again. It rarely happens this way. If this is you, do yourself a favor and take a tip from Denise Linn, which I have passed on to many people with tremendous results. Throw all these clothes away and go out and buy yourself something that makes you look and feel really good exactly as you are now. And guess what usually happens? You lose weight. Call it Sod's Law if you like, but it works, and the reason is that you have stopped resisting being overweight. You have decided to love yourself exactly as you are instead of waiting until you lose weight. What you resist persists, and when you stop resisting, it stops persisting!

A load of old cobblers

We've looked at clothes, but shoes deserve a mention on their own account. Shoes form the foundation of what you wear, and a good pair of shoes can literally make or break a good outfit. Piles of old shoes cluttering up your home are very unsightly and definitely drag the energy down rather than enhance it. Keep the shoes you wear well polished and in good repair and throw away the rest.

Handbags and pockets

How can your life flow freely if you are carrying a handbag with you everywhere you go that is full of all kinds of receipts, used tissues, candy wrappers, and so on? If you would feel embarrassed at the thought of somebody emptying the contents of your handbag onto a table for public examination, empty it out yourself right now and clear out the clutter.

The same advice applies to pants pockets!

OTHER CLUTTER ZONES

Clutter in the car

If you have cleared the clutter in your home but are still driving around knee-deep in garbage, there's still work to do! Your car is like a small world unto itself. Do you cringe and apologize for the state of it whenever you give someone a lift? How many times a week do you think to yourself, "This car really could do with a good cleaning"?

Every time you think about it, your energy dips, until eventually it is costing you more energy not to do it than to just roll up your sleeves and get on with it. You know how good it feels when it has been freshly cleaned out. Treat yourself!

Clutter in the office

Is your desk barely visible beneath a mountain of paperwork? If so, you probably feel defeated before you even start work. Some people protest that they can never find anything if they put it away, or if they don't leave it on their desk they may forget to do it. In Declan Treacy's book, *Clear Your Desk!,* he cites studies that show that the average office worker in the United Kingdom has a backlog of over forty hours of paperwork at any one time and spends about twenty-two minutes each day looking for lost documents because filing or paperwork is not up to date. Those twenty-two minutes a day add up to a staggering four hundred working days over a lifetime! An old folk proverb holds the key, "A place for everything, and everything in its place," so you can always find things when you want them. That way you can always work with a clear desk, which means you will be much more productive.

Many people end up working in a tiny space that is about the size of a piece of paper because the rest of the desk is taken up by piles of paperwork and pieces of equipment. This is so confining! Working with a clear desk increases productivity, creativity, and job satisfaction. An excellent habit to acquire is always to leave your desk clear whenever you finish work. It is psychologically far more uplifting to start work each morning with a clear desk than to come in to mounds of paperwork.

Businesses worldwide use over fifteen million miles of paper every day. That is a lot of paper. The challenge is keeping it under control, and the trick is to ruthlessly throw away as much as possible as often as you can. When Marks and Spencer went through all their files during "Operation Simplification" in the 1950s, they dumped twenty-six million pieces of nonessential paperwork and sold off one thousand filing cabinets that were no longer needed!

There is a day called International Clear Your Desk Day, which takes place on the last Friday in April of every year and is dedicated to clearing clutter from desks. Even if you don't work for a large corporation that participates in this scheme, you can still join in all by yourself. The collective energy generated by everyone else around the world doing it will give you a head start on the job. If you use a computer, you may need to rename this Clear Your Disk Day! Go through your data files and delete old files that are cluttering up your hard disk or copy them to an ordered system of floppy disks. Electronic clutter is just as much of a problem as the more tangible variety.

Many people use message pads or, worse still, post-it notes, to remind themselves to do things. Very soon the work area becomes cluttered with dozens of reminders of things not yet done, and the mind feels burdened. Clear the clutter from your message areas. Use them only for things that are current. If you want to remind yourself to do something, put it in your diary or on a calendar. Post-it notes clutter your mind and make you more likely to forget to do it! Lots of reminders to do things dissipate your energy.

Centralize your information. I have a laptop computer that goes with me wherever I go in the world and a small notebook that I use in my day-to-day work. I have a series of similar notebooks, which I have used over the years. I jot down my answering machine messages, details of telephone conversations and meetings, ideas for workshops I will teach, odd bits of interesting information that come my way, lists of "Things to Do," and so on. I use different colored pens, and every so often I go through the pages with a highlighter pen and highlight key words so that I can easily find information I am looking for. Phone numbers and important information get transferred to my laptop.

Richard Branson also has a notebook he carries with him everywhere and uses for the same purposes, although his version is apparently a larger, more macho volume, and his collection occupies a large shelf! He is reputed to speak to each of his key executives around the world (and there are more than eighty of them) every week, which allows him to keep his finger right on the pulse of what is happening and saves him from having to wade through piles of boring reports. Anita Roddick is another strong proponent of the paper-free office, and so are many other successful entrepreneurs.

Keeping your desk free of clutter begins with how you approach your work in your mind, and here's one sure-fire recipe for success. Charles Schwab, who was the president of the Bethlehem Steel Company in the 1930s, employed a time management consultant, Ivy Lee, to shadow him for two weeks and then advise him on how he could improve his business. The report, when it came, consisted of just three recommendations:

1. Make a list of "Things to Do" every day.
2. Prioritize everything on that list.
3. Tackle things in order of decreasing payoff.

"Don't pay me now," said Ivy Lee, knowing that this succinct advice was a far cry from the usual one-hundred-page reports Schwab received. "Just put my advice into practice for a month and then pay me what it is worth to you." The story goes that one month later, Schwab sent Ivy Lee a check for $25,000—an incredible sum of money in those days. His company went on to become the largest independent steel producer in the world, and in later life he declared that this was the most valuable piece of business advice he had ever received.

Whether you are a million-dollar executive or look after a small suburban home, this advice holds equally true. Try it for a month and see for yourself!

I frequently hear from people that their businesses take off after they clear the clutter in their offices. They may lose a few days' work while they are doing it, but it soon pays for itself many times over! One recent example is a recruitment consultant who came to my workshop, and the next day he went to work and completely cleared his desk. A few days later he clinched a big contract he had been working on for ages but that had proved elusive. Another man reported such a marked increase in turnover after clearing out the clutter in his office that he achieved his goal to reduce his workweek from five to three days and was still able to generate the income he required.

DIFFERENT KINDS OF CLUTTER

Books

Many people find it very hard to let go of books. Holding on to old books doesn't allow you to create space for new ideas and ways of thinking to come into your life. You can become set in your ways and develop musty energy like the musty old books you surround yourself with. Learn to let them go. If this feels too final for you, give your old books to your local library and then, if you ever need to refer to them again, simply borrow them back for a week!

Photos

Do you have drawers or albums stuffed full of photos? Enjoy your photos while they are current. Make colorful montages, put them on the wall, put them in your wallet, stick them on your notebooks, make postcards and send them to your friends. Really get the most from them while their energy is fresh and new. Some people keep photos of all their ex-lovers and then wonder why they have such a hard time finding a new relationship. Or they keep photos that remind them of tough times in the past. Keep the photos that make you feel good and let the rest go. Clear the space for something new and better in your life.

Collections

People sometimes ask me whether collections of things count as clutter. It depends. When you collect something, what you are doing is collecting a particular essence of something that you feel you need. I know one lady who collects dogs. When you go into her home, you are greeted by two huge statues of dogs. There are miniatures of dogs on tables and dressers, and pictures and paintings of dogs everywhere you look in her home and where she works. The only thing that is missing is a real live dog. She had a pet when she was a little girl, and it died in very sad circumstances, which she never got over. The dog collection is a message from her subconscious mind that says, "Take a look at this. It needs your attention. It is a really big issue in your life." When she finally heals the hurt, she will make a tremendous leap forward.

Most people collect something. It's something we naturally do. I think the important thing about collections is to find out why you are doing it and then move on. If you collect frogs, realize there is life beyond frogs. Don't limit yourself. There will come a time when you know in your heart of hearts that your froggy days are over. If you really can't bear to part with all of them, keep your very best frog and march the rest out the door! Make space for something new to come into your life.

Things that need fixing

If there is anything in your home that needs fixing, this is an energy drain too. Your conscious mind has long ceased to notice that chair in the corner with the wobbly leg or that electrical appliance that overheats every time you plug it in, but your subconscious mind remembers exactly, and every time you walk into that room or see an object in your life that reminds you of it, your energy drops.

One woman I know lives in a big house where just about everything in it needs fixing in some way. She does admittedly live on a low income with a child to support, but she is a resourceful, capable woman who could fix things if she wanted to. The lack of care and respect that she has for her home reflects the lack of care and respect she has for herself. When you care for your home by looking after it, you are loving and respecting yourself.

Think of fixing things and improving things in your home as being an investment in yourself. And if there is something you can't be bothered to fix, then toss it or find it a new home with someone who would like it and is willing to repair it.

On certain days in Germany people put out things they don't want and other people take them if they can use them. I think this is a wonderful idea, but if you are caught doing this in England you are likely to be fined!

Other people's clutter

Sometimes people don't have much clutter of their own, but they agree to look after things for other people. "Please look after this ugly sofa for me while I visit New Zealand." Two years later you are still waiting for your friend to come back, and the sofa has started to grow roots!

Think carefully before you agree to clutter your own space, and if you do decide to do it, at least put a time limit on it: "OK, I'll look after your ugly sofa, but if you're not back for it within X months, it's firewood." Make a clear agreement what will happen to the sofa, and that way your friendship won't deteriorate if things don't go according to plan.

Clutter hoarded by a partner

Sometimes an issue like this can bring deep-seated differences to the forefront (which have been buried in the clutter for years and years) that need to be dealt with. Many people take my workshop and then reappear a month or two later with a partner in tow whom they want to hear the information about clutter!

DEEPER LEVELS OF CLEARING CLUTTER

Clear your communications

If you have physical clutter in your home, you will also have mental clutter in your mind. Whom do you have unresolved issues with? Think for a moment. Imagine yourself in a social setting. Are there people in your life who, if they were to walk in the door, would immediately change how comfortable you feel? Who would make you feel that the room wasn't big enough for the two of you, because there are tensions between you? You may not consciously remember these people, in fact you may actively try to keep them out of your thoughts, but your good old subconscious mind keeps track of them. Having unresolved communications in your life depletes your energy levels immensely. If you sleep with someone, make especially certain that you keep your communications clear; otherwise, you will be fighting psychic battles with each other all night and will wake up feeling like you need a good night's sleep.

Clear out your flaky friends

While you are at it, give some attention to clearing out unproductive relationships in your life. Do you have friends whom it always feels like an effort to talk to or who drain you when you are with them? Do you groan when you know so-and-so is calling to talk to you on the phone? I'm not talking here about good friends who are temporarily going through a rough patch or having a bad week! I am talking about negative people who are seriously past their "sell-by-date," who you would like to be rid of but haven't had the guts to or haven't gotten around to doing anything about it. There are billions upon billions of people in the world, and you are free to select whom you choose to associate with. Choose kindred spirits who uplift and inspire you.

The wonderful thing about having the courage to clear out all your moldy old friends (or even your moldy old partner) is that it creates the space for you to attract wonderful, vital new relationships, providing you have made new decisions about what you will and will not have in your life. Eventually you will find that flaky people, energy vampires, and seriously negative individuals will not be in your life because your energy field feels too incompatible with their own—they know that their chances of getting a free energy fill-up at your expense are nil, so they don't even bother trying.

Write those letters

Do you have letters you keep meaning to write but never get around to? Every time you think about it and don't do it, your vitality levels drop. The longer you put it off the more difficult it becomes to write the letter. If you just sit down and take the time to catch up on your correspondence, you will release huge amounts of energy for other purposes.

Tying up loose ends

Get into the habit of tying up loose ends as you go. As an example, sup-posing you are talking with a friend who has a useful telephone number for you. The friend offers to call you with it tomorrow. It's amazing how often people put off until tomorrow what they can quite easily do today, and how much of an energy drain it is having loose ends to remember. Take the phone number then and there, and that is one less thing you have to do in your life!

Keep yourself up to date

When everything is up to date in your life, you live in present time and can experience a real feeling of surfing with the energy of life. Bring your tax returns up to date, and anything else that is nagging away in the back of your mind to be done.

Clear out your colon

A natural progression of clearing clutter in your home is clearing clutter in-side the temple of your own physical body. Look into herbal colon cleans-ing programs. Even if you have been a vegetarian for many years, you will still benefit. If you want to know if you need to do colon cleansing, try the sunflower seed test. Put a handful of sunflower seeds in your mouth, chew them as little as possible, and then swallow them. Now wait until they ap-pear at the other end! If your intestinal transit time is ten or twelve hours, you are in good shape. If it is longer, you could use some colon cleansing to clear the encrustation. Some people may find they have to wait several days before the sunflower seeds appear!

Herbal colon cleansing usually takes six to nine months and needs to be done in conjunction with a regenerative nutrition program. It is always best to work with a qualified herbalist, because clearing the colon invariably brings up emotional issues that you may need support with. Never use laxatives. They irritate and weaken the bowel. Colonic irrigation is useful as an aid to cleansing the body during fasting but is no substitute for the deep cleansing and rebuilding properties of colon herbs. I have included a list of useful books to read on this subject in the Bibliography section at the back of the book, and in the Resources section there are the names of some suppliers of Dr. Christopher's herbal formulas, which are the ones I have found to be most effective.

PRACTICAL STEPS TO CLEARING CLUTTER

If reading all this has inspired you to ninja through your home and zap your clutter to kingdom come, that's great! If you have so much clutter you feel you don't even know where to begin, here are a few pointers to get you started.

- If you are reading this book at home, put it down at the end of this chapter and take a few minutes to walk from room to room taking a mental note of any clutter you need to clear and what you want to do with it. If you are not at home (or are lazy!), just close your eyes and visualize yourself walking from room to room. You will find you know exactly where your clutter is. Remember, if you haven't used it in the last year or two and you don't absolutely love it, then it's time to move it on its way. Sell it, exchange it, toss it, burn it, give it away, or whatever else may be appropriate.

- Decide to clear out just one drawer. Don't overwhelm yourself by intending to clear your whole house or a whole room at once. Do one drawer and, if you want to, go on and do another. Most people find after clearing one drawer, they feel pretty good, and they decide to do another, and maybe another. You can clear your whole house small segments at a time. Adopt the attitude that you will treat yourself to clearing out a drawer! Later, when you have experienced the benefits, you will want to treat yourself more often! As one woman said to me, "I never realized one could get as much pleasure from getting rid of material possessions as from acquiring them in the first place!"

- As you are sorting through what you want to keep and what you want to throw away, don't ask yourself, "Will this come in handy some day?" The answer to this question will always be "maybe," which means that you will never throw anything away. A more productive way is to ask yourself the question: "What does this do for me? Does it lift my energy or does my energy drop when I think about it or look at it?" Use this as your guideline for whether it stays or goes. When your home is filled with objects you love, it becomes an incredible source of nourishment for you. Things you really love have a strong, vibrant energy field around them, whereas things such as unwanted presents have uneasy, conflicting energies attached to them, which drain you rather than energize you.

- If you know you are prone to hoarding, make a new rule for yourself: "When something new comes in, something old goes out." At least your clutter will be changing, even if it's not decreasing yet!

- If you have a lot of clutter, you may need to go through it several times before you feel ready to let go of some things. In some cases, it may take a whole year before you finally get the point that it still hasn't come in handy for anything!

- Empty the garbage pails in your home daily, either at the end of each day or first thing in the morning, whichever suits you best. And make sure you have enough of them around the place so that when you want to toss something you can.

- Affirm to yourself: "It's safe to let go." Clearing clutter is about letting go and trusting the process of life to bring you what you need rather than keeping things "just in case."

•   Realize that everything you own has a hold on your attention. The more clutter you have, the more your energy is tied up in mundane matters. Clear out your clutter to leave yourself free to really make a difference in the world.

The final word on clutter

I was in a taxi the other day, on my way to teach a workshop. The driver and I started chatting, and he asked me what I teach. Rather than blindside him with "Creating Sacred Space with Feng Shui" I simply said that I teach people to clear clutter.

"That's terrific," he enthused. "I used to be a clutterholic, but I went through everything I owned last year and cleared half of it out. My house feels so much better, and my mind feels clearer too, like I can think better. My health has improved as well because I don't get as many colds now as I used to. I always used to get really congested every winter, but since I cleared out my house, I've been fine!"

I sat astonished at the unexpected pearls of wisdom being dropped in my lap.

"It's like a disease, isn't it?" he continued, not waiting for a reply. "You've got to be strict with yourself about what you buy, and you've got to have regular clearouts, because if you don't it will lie in your closets forever. If you don't do something with it, no one else is going to, are they?"

He should be teaching the workshop instead of me, I was thinking to myself by now! He had a way of getting straight to the heart of the matter.

"Yes," he finally concluded his monologue, "I think I'll finish clearing out the other half of my clutter this weekend. It's long overdue!"

6.

Preparation for Space Clearing

NOTES

- *Read all the chapters in Part One of this book before Space Clearing for the first time.*

- *The techniques taught in this book are suitable only for personal use in homes or workspaces. See the important note on page 109 and the "Workshops, Trainings, Consultations, and Special Interest Trips in Bali" section at the end of this book if you are interested in training as a practitioner.*

WHY PREPARATION IS IMPORTANT

The better your preparation, the better your end result will be. I usually reckon that at least 50 percent of the work is in the preparation. If it is done skillfully, and with a good heart and intention, then the effect of the Space Clearing is deep, powerful, and long lasting.

The first time you do Space Clearing, it may be best to do most of the preparation beforehand so that your energy is fresh and vital when you come to do it.

This chapter contains a point-by-point checklist of the most important items that need to be attended to to ensure the best results, and the chapters in Part Two of the book go into more depth about each of the different methods of purification that can be used.

1. Do not attempt Space Clearing if you feel any fear or apprehension.

These techniques are perfectly safe but are designed for personal, everyday use, not for the purposes of exorcism—leave that to trained professionals.

SELF-PROTECTION

One of the first questions that comes to people's minds when they think about learning Space Clearing is that of self-protection, and it certainly was uppermost in mine when I began twenty years ago. At that time, I always used to protect myself by using energy shields, and I have included information about this in Step 6 of the next chapter so that you can use shields if you feel you need to while you are learning. However, I never use them myself now, and I would encourage you not to either because you don't really need them. I realized long ago that nothing can stick to you unless you have something in you that it can mesh with, and you invite it in, consciously or unconsciously.

To give an analogy, supposing someone calls you stupid. If you already believe you are stupid, you will accept their comment. If you think you are stupid but don't like to admit it, you will get upset and react. But if you know you *aren't* stupid, the comment will simply be like water off a duck's back for you. It will have no effect on you at all, because there is nothing in you that their words can mesh with.

Fear or invitation are the routes through which something can come into you. The things you fear are the things you attract to yourself. Unconsciously you invite them into your space. This explains why dogs often seem to go for people who are afraid of them and why many people get the diseases they are most afraid of getting.

So let your feelings be your guide. If you feel any fear or apprehension, your intuition will be alerting you to the fact that you may be taking on too much. If you decide to Space Clear your own home, or the home of a relative or friend, and you don't feel quite right about it, *listen to that feeling*. It means that's not a space you can clear yourself—you need to get help with it or not do it at all. However, it very rarely happens like that. Most places are fine.

"GOOD" AND "BAD" ENERGY

Some people get concerned that by Space Clearing their homes, they will be releasing "bad vibes" into the surrounding neighborhood that may affect others. Space Clearing is about clearing stuck energy and raising the level of vibration in a place. It is not "good" energy or "bad" energy, just as dust and cobwebs are not good or bad—but they are undesirable if you want your home to be fresh and clean. Space Clearing addresses the problem of invisible psychic "debris." It is just static energy that needs to be dispersed and set in motion again. Moving energy is healthy energy, so as soon as you disperse stuck energy, it starts moving again and is therefore not harmful to others.

Other people get concerned that Space Clearing clears out happy memories as well as unhappy ones, but it doesn't work like this. Space Clearing clears out the heavier levels of vibrations that unhappy memories are attached to and leaves the higher levels intact. Actually it enhances the higher levels even more because the lower levels are not weighing them down.

2. *Obtain permission before doing Space Clearing in someone else's personal space.*

PUBLIC BUILDINGS

I never ask permission to Space Clear a public hall or other kind of building, because I reckon I am doing a public service! But it is a very different matter when it comes to clearing the energy in someone's personal space.

PRIVATE HOMES

Having your home Space Cleared can be a very intimate experience, and some people have a very emotional reaction to it. The reason is that it does bring about such incredible changes.

Suppose you decide you'd like to do your grandmother a favor, so you go to her house and you Space Clear it. Realize that she may not thank you for it, because after you've finished it's not going to feel like home to her. It's going to feel like she's been given a completely fresh start, and she may not want that at all! Elderly people often get a bit stuck in their ways, and the energy around them starts to stick too. If you ask them they will often say, "Well, I like my life the way it is, thank you very much," and that is why they often get into fierce battles if, for example, they are urged to relocate to improve their lives. For them it would be a tremendous upheaval, which they don't want to make.

I never do Space Clearing unless I am invited to do it and I am sure the person wants to change. I always insist on dealing with the person responsible for the overall energy of the household. If this is shared between two people (say, a husband and wife), then I am happy to do the consultation with either or both of them. But I never agree to Space Clear a house where the son or daughter asks me to do it without their parents knowing. This would feel entirely wrong to me. And it never works if someone arranges a consultation as a present for someone else, unless that someone else calls to book the session themselves and is there when it happens.

If you share your home with others, you will need to take them into account.

SPACE CLEARING SPECIFIC ROOMS

Sometimes people ask me if it is possible to Space Clear some rooms and not others in a house? Yes, you can Space Clear and exclude certain rooms. If, for example, a particular room in a house is your personal space and you want to clear just that one room, you can do that. Or if you rent out a room in your home and you feel it would be an invasion of your tenant's privacy to Space Clear his or her room, you can exclude that room. If someone is very ill and cannot be taken out of the home, you can (and should) exclude that room temporarily. See point 3, below, for further information about this.

However, unless there are specific circumstances, it is generally better to Space Clear the whole house at the same time, because this encourages the energy to flow evenly around the space.

OFFICES

As far as offices are concerned, it is fine to Space Clear your own office, but I would consider it inappropriate to Space Clear your boss's office and other enclosed areas without permission, because this would be interfering in other people's personal space. As far as open-plan offices are concerned, you must use your own discretion. Just be sure that you never do Space Clearing with the intention of manipulating the energy for your own uses. Do it from the standpoint of wanting to create the highest possibility for everyone who works there.

3. *Do Space Clearing when you feel physically fit, healthy, and emotionally centered.*

You need to be reasonably physically fit, healthy, and emotionally centered to do Space Clearing—but there's no need to wait until you are "perfect" before you begin! It is, however, better to do Space Clearing when your energy is "up." In other words, if you've just had "one of those days" and your energy is down in the dumps, or you've just had a big argument with your partner and your energy is all over the place, it's best to wait until you feel more like yourself.

IF YOU ARE SICK

It's a chicken and egg situation when you are ill. Space Clearing your home can really help the healing process, but you need to be fit and well to do it in the first place. The best thing to do if your health is below par is to enlist the help of a friend.

Having said that, I've heard from people who've been chronically ill and have taken my workshop and decided to do their own Space Clearing. They tell me that, provided they pace themselves and they do a little bit at a time when they feel their energy is "up," it works fine, and the effect is that it actually helps them recover. The next time they find they can do a little bit more, and so on. Space Clearing clears out the old energy, which aids their recovery.

IF OTHERS ARE SICK

The energy fields of physically or mentally sick people are weak or disturbed, so always take them out of the place before you do Space Clearing. If they are too ill to leave the building, you can temporarily shield their room off and exclude it (see the later section on Shielding), then later move them to another room while you Space Clear their room. Remember to take the shields down when you have finished, otherwise they will start to feel very isolated from everyone else in the place!

For less seriously ill people, I still recommend that they leave for a few minutes while you are doing the clapping, but it is often beneficial to their healing process to come back when you begin work with the bells and to witness the rest of the ceremony, providing you explain to them what you are doing.

4. *It is best not to do Space Clearing if you are pregnant, menstruating, or have an open flesh wound.*

MENSTRUATING AND BLEEDING

Let me say straight off that this is nothing to do with women having "the curse," or anything like that. It is because of the blood element, which can apply to both men and women alike.

In many religions, women are not allowed into temples when they are menstruating. Feminists get indignant at this, but perhaps they wouldn't if they really understood the underlying reasons. In Bali, it is not just menstruating women who are not allowed into temples but anyone who is bleeding in any way at all.

One reason is that blood attracts lower levels of entities, and the Balinese don't want those entities in the temple because they want to keep it as clean and pure as possible. Western studies of groups of people who go into jungles or into places far from civilization have shown that if ever they are set upon by wild animals, it is the menstruating women they go for first, and their second choice is anyone with an open flesh wound! Exactly the same thing happens in the realms of energy where lower levels of entities are concerned.

Another completely different reason why menstruating women in particular are not allowed into temples is because they are not able to handle the high levels of energy in temples while their bodies are involved in the monthly process of internal cleansing. All their energies are turned inward, and this is a time when their life force is at its lowest ebb. Women lose life-force energy through menstruation in the same way that men lose it through ejaculation.

Space Clearing is about cleansing externally, and women are not equipped to do this so well at the time of the month they are doing their own internal electromagnetic cleansing. I used to sometimes do Space Clearing when I had my period, but I found I got a lesser result and I felt more exhausted afterward. Nowadays I never do Space Clearing when I have my period, and I certainly wouldn't do a full-scale consecration cere-mony (described in Chapter 12) while menstruating.

PREGNANCY

Similarly, during pregnancy, a woman's energies are turned inward because they are in the process of building and nourishing a new life inside. Also, everything that happens to the mother is transmitted directly to the sensi-tive fetus inside her. To protect the child and nourish the mother, preg-nancy is a time for a woman to have her partner do Space Clearing for her. In ancient cultures women would go into "confinement" during the time they were pregnant, which was for the entire gestation period, not just for a few hours while they were in labor. From the time they conceived, they would live in the elevated atmosphere of a specially created place apart from other members of the tribe to give that new life the best possible op-portunity. They knew that the most formative time in a person's life was the time spent in the womb.

If you are pregnant, you can use many of the tips in Part Two of this book to enhance your own atmospheres and purify yourself, but it is best to leave the basic Space Clearing procedures to someone else, especially the more heavy-duty aspects such as the clapping techniques I will de-scribe later.

5. Take the time to think about what you want to have happen in your life. If you share the space with others, it is best to consult them too.

CLARITY OF INTENTION

If you Space Clear without having thought about what you want to fill the space with next, it will work, but the space usually just starts to fill up with more of the same stuff again in the days and months that follow.

It is best to give the matter some thought before you begin, and—bet-ter still—to sit down with a pen and paper and write a description of what you would like your life to be like. You can do this in the form of a point-by-point list or as a narrative. Be as specific as you can, and at the end of it write: "May this or something better now manifest for the highest good of everyone concerned," then sign and date it. This last sentence is to create an opening for the universe to manifest something better than you may have thought of and to ensure that the process benefits everyone, not just you.

6. For best results, physically clean and straighten up the space, sweep, mop or vacuum it, and clear out clutter first.

Clearing out clutter is such an important topic that the whole of the last chapter was devoted to it.

The best time to do Space Clearing is after a good spring cleaning. If your place is in such a state (reflecting the state of your life) that you can't face doing all this first, then at least take the time to sweep, mop, or vacuum the place before Space Clearing.

SWEEPING

Soon after dawn in Bali, the swishing sound of rhythmic, methodical sweeping fills the air. It is somehow restful, comforting, and does not disturb your sleep but rather adds a new dimension to it. They are using stiff brushes made from coconut leaf spines.

This is happening everywhere on the island. Every piece of land near human habitation and every home, building, and temple is swept clean at the start of every day and at intervals throughout the day as required. Purification is such an intrinsic part of this remarkable culture that it is no surprise that this fundamental practice is so deeply ingrained into the way of life. In temples, special brooms exclusive to sacred areas are used, and each temple has an attendant who looks after such matters.

HIGH- AND LOW-LEVEL ENERGIES

In understanding how sweeping purifies a space by clearing out lower levels of energy, it is necessary to understand that high energy collects in high-level places, and low energy collects in low-level places. This is why many great spiritual cultures in the world have been located at the tops of mountains. It is also why penthouse suites are so sought after, because the people living there have an energetic advantage over people living at lower levels. People who live up on mountains are generally happier and more optimistic than people who live in valleys, where the energy tends to collect and coagulate. Valley people tend to experience more struggle in their lives and are more likely to experience depression. It is much easier to feel elated on top of a mountain.

In buildings, low energy collects at floor level and high energy collects at higher levels. This is recognized in Bali by the attention paid to relative seating positions. It is always arranged that priests sit higher than common folk, and if someone is having a conversation with a priest and the priest sits down, the person of lower status must do likewise so that he is not placing himself in a more elevated position. Tourists sometimes scramble up onto temple walls to try to get the perfect photo, not realizing they are committing a cardinal sin by putting themselves higher than the officiating priest. The Balinese take a very dim view of this obvious ignorance of such matters.

In terms of the human body, low energy emanates from the feet and high energy from the head. This is easy to understand in terms of the chakras of the human body, which are seven energy vortexes located up the central meridian of the body. They range from the base chakra at the base of the spine up to the crown chakra at the top of the head, and many traditional yogic healing and meditation techniques are based on the fact that there is a definite progression of energy refinement from base to crown chakra. Highly developed souls have a radiation around the head, which we call a halo and which can be seen in religious paintings of all religions and cultures. In Bali, buildings are traditionally never built more than one-story high, simply because no one wants to put themselves in the position of having someone else's feet above their head!

In many Southeast Asian cultures shoes are left at the door when entering a building, and in some temples all footwear is strictly forbidden. One reason for this is that footwear is always in contact with the ground and is also impregnated with the lower emanations of the feet. In temples, removing footwear also allows the sacred energy of the place to enter directly through the soles of a person.

In most Eastern religions, there are also taboos about where feet can be pointed, especially in temples. The feet must never be pointed toward sacred objects, altars, and so on. Balinese people are very sensitive to the lower levels of emanations from the feet. In everyday life, it is considered highly insulting to sit with your feet directly pointing toward another person.

Reflexologists would do well to take note of this information. Western practitioners often work with the patient's foot resting in their laps and pointing toward them. Many of them become very unwell and are especially likely to develop stomach problems. I have noticed that skillful practitioners in Bali always work by laying the patient down and sitting alongside them and facing toward their feet so that low-level energies that are released during the healing session disperse freely and do not become absorbed into the stomach of the person giving the treatment.

VACUUMING

Vacuum cleaners are the modern equivalent of sweeping and can be used as appropriate. In fact, if your room needs a quick pick-me-up and you don't have time to go through all the Space Clearing procedures, a quick once-over works wonders! But don't get obsessive about this. One woman I knew used to vacuum so many times a day that the atmospheres in her home became raw and sensitive, and she became so touchy she would bite your head off if you put a word (or a foot) out of place!

Therapists find that vacuuming before sessions really helps to perk their energy levels up, and it sometimes helps to vacuum between clients, especially if you have had a difficult or intense session.

7. *Take a full bath or shower, or at least wash your face and hands.*

Water is a great cleanser and purifier, both physically and energetically. It is very important to feel clean and fresh before you begin Space Clearing, and you will also be able to sense energy better too. If you have done major cleaning and straightening up beforehand, you are bound to feel grimy and dirty. It is best to take a full bath or shower, including washing your hair and brushing your teeth, and then put on clean clothes. You will get a much better result.

8. *Put food and drink away in cupboards or sealed containers.*

It is good to drink lots of water while you are Space Clearing to help your own energies move more easily, but don't pour yourself a glass of water, do the Space Clearing, and then drink the glass of water at the end! I have done it once or twice without thinking, and the water tastes brackish and foul. Water is a wonderful purifier, and it will naturally absorb some of the stuck energy you disperse while you are Space Clearing. Most other kinds of food and drink (anything with any water content except fruit, which is sealed tight inside its own skin) will do so too if you leave them in the open. Put it all away in cupboards, in the refrigerator, or in sealed containers of some sort.

9. Remove jewelry and other metallic objects from your person. Work barefoot if possible.

ABOUT JEWELRY

Jewelry was originally worn in ancient cultures not as decoration but to enhance people's energy fields as they progressed through different levels of personal development. So if they were maintaining their energy body at the frequency of, say, silver, they would wear silver jewelry to help them do that. If they were doing a sacred dance at the level of gold, they would wear gold jewelry to accentuate the energy that came out of their body, particularly their hands and feet. There are highly sensitive acupressure points on the fingers, wrists, upper arms, ankles, toes, neck, earlobes, and so on. The costumes of Balinese dancers today still portray in precise detail the winged developments that occur in the aura of a highly developed person, and similar illustrations can be seen in art from Egypt, India, and other great cultures of the world.

Space Clearing is initially about clearing energy out rather than flavoring it in any particular way, so it is best to do this without wearing any jewelry at all. Also metallic jewelry acts as an electrical conductor, which can pick up static energy while you are working. After clearing the building, you may be faced with extra work to purify yourself and clear your jewelry if you don't remove it before you start. A wedding ring that won't come off can be a disadvantage in this work. If this is your situation, see the section, Purification by Water, in Chapter 9, for how to cleanse your ring, and take a salt water bath after Space Clearing to purify yourself.

WATCHES

It is always a good idea to take your watch off when you are Space Clearing. Apart from the fact that watches have metal components that can cause the same problems as jewelry, Space Clearing can sometimes cause them to malfunction or stop altogether. I have had many different kinds of watches in my life and have now completely given up wearing them because they all break on me pretty quickly. I have the same effect on radio microphones and other electronic gadgets that are supposed to be worn on the body. I'm not sure exactly why this is, but it has something to do with the huge amounts of energy I process in my work. It may not happen to you, but it might. Another reason why it is best to take your watch off is because you can sense energy better without anything on your wrists.

METAL-FRAMED EYEGLASSES

If you can manage without them, it is preferable to take them off while you are Space Clearing, especially if the frames have a metal piece across the nose (the study of acupuncture shows that this can short-circuit the energy meridians of the head, which can cause tiredness, confusion, and headaches even in normal everyday circumstances).

COINS

Empty any coins out of your pockets before beginning Space Clearing.

OTHER METALLIC OBJECTS

Remove any other metallic objects such as belts with metal buckles.

ABOUT BEING BAREFOOT

It is best to do Space Clearing barefoot because you can feel the energy so much better that way. A lot of information comes in through the soles of the feet, both from the ground itself and from the floors of the building. Shoes insulate you from feeling that, especially shoes with soles made from artificial materials. If you need to, put on shoes to go into areas such as dirty basements and then take them off again when you come out. If you are doing Space Clearing in winter, wear cotton socks or leather-soled slippers to keep your feet warm if necessary—there is no point being barefoot if your feet are like blocks of ice and you can't feel them!

1 0 .   *Work alone unless other people present fully understand what you are doing.*

DOING SPACE CLEARING ALONE

When I first started doing Space Clearing, I never used to do it with any-one else around. I would ask everyone to leave the house for as long as it took and then invite them back in when the job was done. I suggest that you do this too.

Space Clearing moves energy, including energy in people if they are in the space. If they do not understand what you are doing, and they start to feel unfamiliar shifts of energy inside themselves, they can react with fear, distress, irritation, and a whole range of other emotions. Some of the procedures look a little strange. They are actually normal everyday actions, but just in an unusual context. You can attempt to explain what you are do-ing as you do it, but then your attention is not fully on the Space Clearing. Until you are very experienced, it is best to work alone or with someone who knows what you're doing.

In my professional work I try to make very sure that everyone present understands and feels comfortable with what I am doing. Of course there have been a few instances where the cleaner has turned up in the middle of the ceremony, and I remember one poor Polynesian woman in particu-lar who spoke hardly a word of English, and it was her first day on the job. She looked terrified when I started clapping, and I thought she was going to bolt out of the door. I smiled reassuringly and put a temporary energy shield around her. She relaxed a bit when she heard the beautiful tone of the bells I use to balance energies and was positively beaming by the time I had finished. It would have been easier to postpone the Space Clearing until another time, but I knew I could make it safe for her.

I have become used to working with whole families following me around. Now that I am experienced in working this way, I will very rarely agree to do Space Clearing if the head of the household is *not* present!

I still find that it is best to Space Clear offices when they are empty, and this is because it is difficult to work with the energy of a place when it is a hive of activity, and it would also take too long to explain to everyone what I am doing. Only the owner, or someone responsible, needs to be present.

DOING SPACE CLEARING WITH A PARTNER

If you have a partner you share your home with, and you would like to share responsibility for the Space Clearing, you may like to do the entire ceremony together. If you want to split the work, do the preparation together, and then it usually works well for the man (or the more *yang* [active] partner) to do the clapping and the shielding and the woman (or the more *yin* [passive] partner) to do the other procedures. This is by no means a hard and fast rule, however. The important thing is to do the bits you most like doing. Wait until your partner has completed his or her part of the process before you commence the next stage.

11. Work in silence without background music. Turn off any fans and other nonessential loud or droning machinery.

MUSIC

A lot of Space Clearing is listening to the way energies reverberate and resonate as you make your way around the room or building, and you can't hear any of this if there are angelic choruses (or heavy rock music) in the background. Music is a wonderful way to create different atmospheres in your home, but is best used *after* Space Clearing.

FANS AND AIR CONDITIONING

I feel physically dizzy, nauseous, and mentally confused if I stand near a fan or air conditioning unit, and I always get an instant headache. They churn up the air and also the energy in a room and in the auric field of anyone who comes near one. They also emit large electromagnetic fields, which can be very draining, and make droning noises, which can cause nervous stress.

Fans in particular create large movements of air, which makes it very difficult to sense energies and also makes it virtually impossible for you to stay centered while you are doing the Space Clearing because your own energy field (your aura) will be dragged all over the place. The effect of air conditioning is generally more subtle but can be more insidious. I always turn air conditioning off in any rooms I am teaching workshops in because it confuses the energy so much that I invariably end up with the flu the next day.

12. Open a door or a window.

Actually energy can travel through solid objects, but when you first begin this kind of work it is reassuring to open a door or window and invite the stuck energy you are dispersing to depart through that gap. We live in physical bodies, and we feel psychologically more comfortable if we leave a door ajar or a window open. However, don't have so much air rushing through that it makes it impossible to sense energies.

13. Locate an appropriate power point and set up your Space Clearing equipment.

POWER POINTS

There are several different kinds of power points in a building. A power point is a place from which you feel that you can connect with every place in the room or building. In a room the power point is usually diagonally opposite the door, so that when you stand there you have a full view of the door and windows of the room. This obviously varies from room to room. Power points of entire buildings vary even more, and your best guide is your intuition.

As far as setting up your Space Clearing equipment is concerned, it is usually best to find a power point just inside the main entrance that has the sense of, "Yes, I can talk to the house from here!" about it. Energy and people enter through the main entrance of your home, so it is best to place yourself as much as possible in the path of that. If the entrance is very narrow, it is usually better to set up "base camp" in the living room if that room is fairly close to the front door, or any other suitable room (not a bathroom or junk room).

Position a small table with enough room around it so that it doesn't obstruct you as you are walking around (there's quite a lot of walking involved in doing Space Clearing thoroughly).

BASIC SPACE CLEARING EQUIPMENT

You will need:

- A tablecloth (preferably one that is only used for special ceremonies or has never been used before)

- Sea salt or rock salt in a sealed container

- Generous quantities of flower heads and petals (choose colors you love and that go well together)

- Nightlight candles in metal holders

- Some small saucers to put the candles and flower heads on

- A few fresh leaves

- Incense and incense holders

- Matches

- Holy water or charged water in a sealed container
  (see Chapter 9)

- A bell or a series of bells with good quality tone
  (see Chapter 8 and the Resources section at the back of the book)

- One or more harmony balls (these will be explained in Step 7 of the next chapter)

Take a little time to arrange your equipment so that it looks pleasing to you. I have a beautiful tablecloth that I use whenever I do Space Clearing, which transforms even the most mundane of tables into a sacred space. If you don't have any of the items on this list, you can still proceed, but the Space Clearing won't be as effective. It may be worth waiting until you can buy, borrow, or be given what you need. Continue reading to discover all the different methods of purification before you make your decisions about what you want to acquire.

14. *Roll up your sleeves and sensitize your hands.*

I seem to live my life with my sleeves permanently rolled up, and probably you will too once you discover how much more you can feel this way. The hands and forearms are very sensitive to energies.

EXERCISE TO SENSITIZE YOUR HANDS

This is one of the practical exercises I have used for years in my workshops, which many people have obtained good results with. You can do it with your eyes open as you read the book, but it works better if you read the passage first and then close your eyes and do it.

Wash your hands and take off any rings, bracelets, watch, and so on. Roll up your sleeves and sit in a comfortable chair with your hands resting in your lap, slightly apart, your palms facing upward. Completely relax your hands and begin to focus your attention on your palms and your fingertips. You may become aware of tiny tingles of electricity on your skin, which is your own electromagnetic energy. Probably you will feel this most intensely in your fingertips, which are constantly radiating energy.

Spend a few minutes feeling this and then raise both hands to waist level and turn your palms to face each other. Curve your palms as if they are holding a very soft imaginary ball about the size of a soccer ball between them. Bounce your palms toward each other as if you are gently squeezing and releasing the ball and feel the sensations of the energy flowing between your two palms.

After you have done this for a few minutes, expand the size of the ball to a modest beach-ball size. The energy may feel a little weaker now, but the connection will still be there.

Now bring your palms close together, to about the size of a tennis ball apart. Continue to bounce the energy, which will feel more intense, perhaps almost physical. Do this for a few minutes. Then, in much the same way that you can "photograph" and remember a visual image with your eyes, take a body photograph so that at a later time you will be able to remember how your hands feel in this sensitized state. As you take the body photograph, it helps to do a "link signal" such as clenching and unclenching a hand, putting one hand on top of your head, or any quick, simple action that you wouldn't normally do in the course of everyday living. You can then repeat this link signal whenever you want to resensitize your hands without having to go through this whole exercise again.

When you feel confident that you have captured the feeling for future use, disengage your hands by turning your palms upward and relaxing them back into your lap.

LEARNING TO SENSE ELECTROMAGNETIC ENERGIES

Do this practical exercise right after the last one for best results. You will need another human being, an animal, or a plant to practice on. It is easier to feel the energy fields of animate beings rather than beginning right away with buildings, and humans and cats are generally the easiest to feel.

If you have a person you can work with, ask them to hold their hands up at arms length in front of themselves, with their palms facing toward you. Do your link signal to reactivate your sensitivity and then, using one or both of your hands, begin to feel the energy coming out of their palms. Register at what distance you can begin to feel it.

If you have a cat or can borrow one, try stroking it from head to tail about six inches away from its fur, following the contours of its body. Cats are very electrical beings. If you do a few stroking motions like this, most will respond by arching their backs as they do when they are physically stroked.

You can also sense the energy fields of plants. Don't attempt this in the open air at this stage unless it is a perfectly still day, because even a slight breeze will make it difficult for you to distinguish the electromagnetic fields.

After completing all these preparations, you are now ready to begin the actual Space Clearing procedures.

7.

Basic Space Clearing Procedures

Every space is different and has different requirements, but there are some procedures that form the basis of all Space Clearing work.

Over the years, I've worked out something I call basic Space Clearing, which is an instant formula you can begin to use immediately in your home. All the feedback I receive from people who take my workshops tells me that this is producing excellent results, so this is the approach I am going to take in presenting the information in this book.

The techniques I am about to describe will assure you of success if you follow the steps in the order I present them. I strongly recommend that you do so. Then, after you have done Space Clearing a few times and have gained confidence through experience, you can add in other enhancements or substitute some of the different techniques I will describe in the following chapters.

THE BEST TIME TO DO SPACE CLEARING

The best time to do Space Clearing is just after you have done your physical housework and during daylight hours if possible. I have also found that all purification work is easier to do and works better between full moon and new moon. It is not such a good idea to do the ceremony just before you go on vacation or go away for a while because you will not be there to receive the full benefit of the process.

Choose a time when you are not likely to be disturbed by neighbors. Take your phone off the hook or switch on your answering machine if you have one. If you have young children, find someone to look after them for a few hours to leave yourself free to focus on what you are doing. Children and babies are very sensitive to energy shifts and may act up while the Space Clearing is going on, which means you would have to stop what you are doing to attend to them.

Most animals like to be around while Space Clearing is going on. They can see the energy and become very interested in watching it move. Pets of a nervous disposition sometimes run away at the clapping stage but will usually return at the bell-ringing stage if you are using a good quality bell.

The length of time it takes to Space Clear your home depends very much on how big it is, how much clutter is in it, what has happened in the space in the past, and whether you naturally work at a quick pace or prefer to go more slowly. In my professional work, I allow an hour for a one- or two-bedroom home and correspondingly more time for larger places. I find it best to keep up a brisk pace so that the energy doesn't have a chance to congeal again before the process is complete!

1. Take time to attune to the space. Mentally announce yourself and radiate your intention.

BREATHING

In Space Clearing you are essentially revitalizing the energy of a building, so it is important that you remember to breathe well throughout the process to keep your own energy moving. If other people are present, make sure they also breathe well too. As the atmosphere becomes clearer and more rarefied, people tend to get so caught up in what is happening that their breathing becomes shallower and shallower, which can make it more difficult to clear the space. Just tell them to take a deep breath if you notice this is happening.

CONNECTING WITH YOUR HOME

Realize that in its housey kind of way, your home has feelings just as you do and will respond to you according to how you treat it. If you honor and respect the space, it will nourish and support you in return.

Also realize that buildings have their own individual personalities. Most people have had the experience of walking into a place and thinking "This feels really nice" or "I wouldn't like to live here." They are connecting with the basic character and energy of the place.

To begin to connect with your home, stand just inside the front entrance, which may mean the front door of your house or the door of your apartment, or the door of your room if you live in part of a house. Take a moment to center yourself by drawing your energies to yourself and visualizing all your chakras in perfect balance. Now focus your attention on the outermost edge of your aura. This pulsating egg-shaped energy field extends all the way around you and can be expanded or contracted at will (the phrase "sleep tight" refers to the way we naturally draw our aura in closer toward our bodies when we go to sleep).

Visualize your aura expanding to fill the entire space of your home. Open your heart chakra (you may like to image it as an unfolding flower, perhaps a beautiful pink one) and allow the love from your heart to flow out into every part of the space too. Mentally announce who you are and what you are intending to do and radiate that intention out into the space.

The first time you do this it may not feel like your home is really receiving the message, but over a period of time you can establish a relationship with it, and you'll probably end up being one of those people who comes home and strokes the walls and says "Hello!" It is possible to build up a very personal relationship with your home. You may like to give it a name to cement that relationship even deeper.

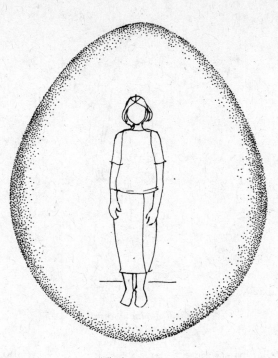

The human aura

2. *Starting at the main entrance, go around the inside perimeter of the space, sensing the energy. Use your hands and all your other senses too.*

ENGAGING WITH THE ENERGY

Now it is time to begin to engage more physically with the energy of your home. Stand sideways, just inside your front door. Face whichever way feels most comfortable to you. Hold the hand nearest the door a few inches away from it with your arm extended at shoulder height and loosely bent at the elbow. Bend your hand at about ninety degrees to your wrist, with your fingers pointing upward and your flat palm facing toward the door. Keep your hand and your arm supple and relaxed.

Now begin to slowly stroke the energy field of the front door. The

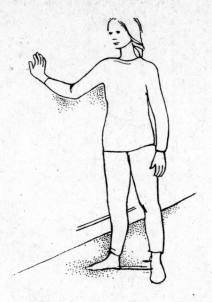

Engaging with the energy

motion is similar to stroking a cat and is done horizontally at shoulder height and toward the way you are facing. Do this several times in a caressing kind of way, all the while radiating your intention to connect with your home for the purpose of purifying your living space. There comes a point when it suddenly feels as if the energy parts, and then the building opens up to you. If you have already been in the habit of stroking or patting the walls or furniture in your home sometimes, the house is already familiar with this and will usually open immediately. People who have an affinity with people, animals, or plants find it very easy to develop an affinity with buildings too.

While you are doing this, hold yourself in a state of open receptivity, listening to the house on all levels. When I do private consultations I often pick up more information in these first few seconds of engagement than in the whole of the rest of the time I am there, but you have to be quick to catch it. One common occurrence is that if the person has been worried about what personal information might come to light when I read the energy of the home, this is reflected in the reticence of the energy of the house to open to me. A few words of reassurance to the owner and it is as if the doors swing wide open!

When Space Clearing your own home, listen for messages. Your home may have wanted to communicate with you for years to let you know what it needs. If you are the kind of person given to flights of fantasy, you may come up with a load of gibberish at this point. It's a fine line between really hearing what your home has to say and hearing what you want to hear. Just approach the whole thing in a matter-of-fact but open-minded kind of way.

After doing the stroking motion a few times and assimilating any information you may pick up on, start to walk slowly forward around the inside perimeter of the space, using your hands and all your other senses.

SENSING THE ENERGY

At first you may not feel very much. Don't worry, because I have designed these basic Space Clearing procedures so that they work perfectly well even if you can't feel a thing! It is actually much easier to feel the electromagnetic pulsations that emanate from living beings before you try to feel the fainter vibrations emanating from buildings, so keep practicing on your friends, pets, and plants to enhance your sensitivity.

When sensing energy in buildings, you may feel like you are putting your hands into anything ranging from gossamer-fine cobwebs to thick, sticky molasses. Some places will feel hot, some cool. Some sensations will be pleasant, and others not so pleasant. You may feel dull aches in your bones or shimmering tingles in your palms. It may feel as smooth as honey or as lumpy as gravel. Remember always to keep in mind that you are not taking any of this "stuff" on board. If you feel like you have picked up some of the stuck energy (stuck energy can be pretty sticky!), it will only be on your hands and possibly your forearms, and it will wash off immediately later. If the sensations are very strong, you may need to shake your hands from time to time to refresh your sensitivity.

CLOCKWISE OR COUNTERCLOCKWISE?

I am often asked, "Does it matter which way you walk around?" When I first started to do this work, I used to walk around counterclockwise to take energy out and clockwise to put energy in. I now know that it actually doesn't matter which way you walk around, because what is important is your intention. It feels more comfortable to me to go counterclockwise, so nowadays I nearly always walk around in that direction, whether I'm clearing the space or putting new energy in. Go whichever way feels most comfortable to you.

WORK FROM THE BOTTOM TO THE TOP

If your home is on more than one story, start at the bottom of the building and move up level by level (energy stacks from the bottom up).

This is straightforward if your entrance is situated on the lowest floor. You simply start inside the front door and go around the inside perimeter of the building until you arrive back at the front door.

If your entrance is on the ground floor and there is a basement below it, follow the inside perimeter around until you reach the entrance to the basement, then go down into the basement, right around the inside perimeter of it (if practically possible - some basements are too cluttered or too awful to go into), then come up, continue around the ground floor and up the stairs to the other floors of the house.

Include the attic if there is one and if there is easy access to it. If access is difficult, don't worry. It's more important to go into basements because so much low level energy collects there, but it is not so important to go into attics. Just visualize the effects of the Space Clearing rising up to fill the space in the roof.

Go all the way around the inside perimeter of the space until you arrive back at the front door.

If it is a very big house, you may choose to do the Space Clearing one floor at a time. In this situation, always do your energy sensing starting at the front door and going around the entire house. Then do the Space Clearing procedures floor by floor, from the bottom up. First do the basement, finish that completely, then do the ground floor, and so on. Include the stairs as part of the next floor up.

In some smaller houses, where different floors are used for very different purposes (for example, one floor is residential and another floor is used by you to run a business) it may also work best to Space Clear floor by floor if you want to keep the energies separate.

Walking around the inside perimeter of your home is a wonderful way to get to know how the energy flows, and it may be a total revelation for you. All Feng Shui is based on harmonizing the flow of energy, and if you have to clamber over obstacles or pick your way through piles of clutter to make your way around, you will appreciate that energy has the same difficulties as you do!

> 3. *Light candles, burn incense, sprinkle holy
> water, and offer flowers and prayers to the
> guardian spirit of the house and the spirits of
> earth, air, fire, and water. Call in the angels and
> your own personal guides and helpers (whatever
> feels appropriate to you).*

There are a number of different ways you can do this, and it is important to find a way that feels right to you. I like to begin by lighting a candle, burning some incense, and placing an offering of flowers sprinkled with holy water (see Chapter 9 for how to make or acquire this) on the table where I have set up my Space Clearing equipment. I then put a line of salt across each threshold of the building, and put more lighted candles, burning incense, and offerings of flowers sprinkled with holy water at key points around the building.

OFFERINGS

To make a flower offering, place a candle in the center of a saucer and arrange freshly picked flower heads around the candle radiating outward. Make the contrasting colors and arrangement of the flowers as abundant and attractive as you can.

If your home has several stories, put at least one such offering on each floor. The living room and master bedroom are the most important places to put them, as well as the kitchen stove, which is where food is cooked to nourish everyone who lives in the home. In Feng Shui, the kitchen stove is considered to be a vital life-enhancing asset, which symbolically represents financial prosperity. The Balinese always place a small offering on the

A flower offering

kitchen stove after cooking and at various other shrines around the house. These consist of small portions of banana leaves with a few grains of cooked rice and tiny pieces of other ingredients of the meal, and they represent miniature meals for the gods, intended as a way of expressing gratitude.

Ideally place offerings in every major room in the house. First lay a small leaf in position and then place the flower offering on top. Put a burning incense stick next to it in an incense holder, then light the candle and use a flower head to flick some holy water onto the offering.

These are offerings to the guardian spirit of the house and the elemental spirits. The flowers represent earth, the incense is for the spirits of the air, the lighted candle is for the element of fire, and the holy water represents the element of water. The candles activate the ceremony and are beacons of light that register in the realms of the unseen, direct the flow of energy, and help to purify the space while you are working.

As you make the offerings and light the candles and incense, hold firmly in your mind the intention you have in performing this ceremony, such as creating a clear space for the next phase of your life to manifest or creating a safe and loving space for you and your family. If you want to offer prayers and invoke blessings, this is the time to do so. You can also extend invitations to angels and your own personal guides and unseen helpers to be present and assist with the ceremony if you are familiar with working in this way.

Take care that the incense and candles can burn safely. Position them well away from curtains and other flammable materials and out of reach of children and animals. I always burn incense in an incense holder, and the safest kind of candles are nightlights in metal containers, placed on heat-resistant saucers. Allow the incense and candles to continue burning after the ceremony until they are completely finished. If you need to go out, extinguish them and relight them when you return home.

4. Clap in corners to disperse static energy. Then wash your hands in running water (very important to remember to do this).

BASIC CLAPPING

Start at the main entrance to the house and go around the inside perimeter of the space, sensing the energy again with your outstretched hand. Every time you come to a corner, stop and give several short claps to disperse the energy.

It is not necessary to clap all the way from the floor to the ceiling, but it does work better if you move up or down the corner as you do it. I prefer to start with my hands slightly above my head and clap downward to about waist level, increasing the intensity of the clapping as I do it. Other people get good results starting low and clapping up to above the head. Whichever method you use, have the intention that the clapping extends up and down the corner and visualize the area as becoming completely clear. Smooth your hand over the area after you have clapped it out to smooth out the energy and then continue around the space, sensing as you go.

Work systematically around the building. Clap out all the corners and all the nooks and crannies. If you feel a "hot-spot" between corners where the energy literally feels hotter than normal, clap that out too. As you move, have the intention that you leave a path of clear energy in your wake.

If you want to be really thorough, open closets and cupboards and clap them out too. Clap around electrical equipment, especially computer monitors, televisions, and other areas where static electricity builds up. You can

Clapping out corners

clap out beds, and the best way to do this is "with the grain," in other words, from the head to the foot of the bed. For large beds you will need to make several passes, clapping as you go. Go right around the space and back to where you first started.

Your clapping will usually sound dull and thuddy at first and will gradually become crisper and clearer. When you are about three-quarters of the way around the building, you may start to hear what I call "after-twang," which is when the clapping starts to reverberate. When you hear this, you know that this particular part of the Space Clearing process is almost complete.

Usually once around is enough to do the job, but if you get back to the place you first started and you can't hear that resonance, you will need to go around a second time and do it again. Maybe you weren't putting enough into it, or maybe there was just a lot to clear. It may all sound the same to you, in which case, don't worry too much. Any clapping is better than no clapping, and once around is probably enough!

EMOTIONAL REACTIONS

In my professional work, it sometimes happens that people have an emotional reaction during the process of clapping out their home, and they may even burst into tears. It is not that they feel sad, it's just part of the process of letting go. It doesn't happen very often, but I include the information here so that you will understand if you start to feel these feelings while you are clearing your own home. Let the tears come if they want to, and help the energy to move by taking deep breaths. It will quickly pass.

DIFFERENT WAYS OF CLAPPING

I have clapped out thousands of rooms in my time and am still amazed at the many different kinds of clapping there are. I may work my way around the rooms of a home clapping at a very slow, sedate pace, and then suddenly come to a bedroom where I feel impelled to clap twice as fast. This tells me that the person who sleeps in that room has a very different character and personal rhythm from the other members of the household, who will probably find him or her hard to understand.

There are many different rhythms you can clap in, and many different intensities and volumes. In large rooms you will probably need to do much louder clapping than in smaller rooms, and you may also find that softer clapping is more appropriate for the rooms of children and babies. You will also find that you feel inclined to clap very firmly in some places and very compassionately in others. This constitutes a whole study in itself, but for basic Space Clearing, just do what feels best to you.

THE CROCODILE CLAP

This is a special clapping technique I have developed specifically for clapping out the narrow space between a closet and a wall, where there is not enough room to do a conventional clap. You put your palms together with one hand flat on top of the other and extend your arms into the narrow space. Then you pull your arms apart like a crocodile opening its jaws and bring them back together again at speed so that your hands clap together!

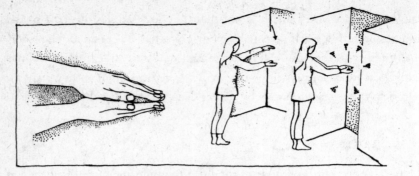

The crocodile clap—for narrow spaces

LONG-DISTANCE CLAPPING

This is a technique I have developed for clapping out grizzly or cluttered basements. I never feel it is as effective as actually getting in there and clapping out each corner individually, but it's reasonably adequate.

What you do is stand at the entrance to the basement and focus your attention on the first corner you want to clap out. As you clap, look at the corner and throw the clap along the beam of your sight into the corner. Then use your eyes to sweep the effect of it up and down the corner. Work around the basement, throwing claps into each corner, nook, and cranny of the space.

WASH YOUR HANDS

It is VERY, VERY important to remember to wash your hands under running water after you have finished clapping. This washes off any bits of psychic debris that may have clung to you, and you will feel fresh and ready to move on to the next stage immediately.

5. Purify the space with bells.

CREATING A SACRED CIRCLE OF SOUND

This will be your third lap of the inside perimeter of the building. Begin by using the bell with the deepest tone you have that is appropriate for the space (larger rooms require deeper tones). Starting inside the front entrance, ring it once, then listen. When you have done this a few times in a few different buildings, you get to know whether you have engaged with the energy of the place the first time or whether you need to ring it again. If in doubt, ring it two or three times.

Next, start to walk around the inside perimeter of the space, holding the bell near to the wall but not so close that you bang it against the wall. Hold it above waist level—on a level with your heart is best. Walk forward, ringing the bell as you go, just enough so that the sound never fades. As you walk, you are creating a sacred circle of sound in your wake. It helps to intensify the effect if you also visualize this as a shining circle of pure shimmering light and sound. You take the clear energy with you, and if you come to a spot where the bell doesn't resound so well, pause and ring the bell again until you get the resonance. If you listen, you can hear where energy collects and stagnates, so you know where to pay special attention in future.

When you get back to the point you started from, draw a horizontal figure eight in the air with the bell. This is the symbol of eternity, which tells the energy "and so on," so that it keeps going around and around the circle you have created. The effect lasts much longer this way.

If, while you are walking around, something distracts your attention, the energy will fall a little flat and you may need to start the whole circle again. With practice you will be able to tell whether you can reengage the energy, but if in doubt, start again.

Then take a smaller bell and do exactly the same again. This will now be the fourth time you have walked around the entire inner perimeter of the house, and when I do consultations in large ancestral mansions it is at this point that I usually start wishing I were being paid a mileage allowance!

In the past I used to use maybe four or five different bells in any one space to get the desired effect, using smaller and smaller bells each time and refining the energy in stages. Then I discovered Bali and Balinese bells. In Chapter 8 you will find the story of how I acquired my first Balinese bell and what is so special about it. I also explain why the Space Clearing methods I describe in this book are only safe if you use a Balinese bell.

HOW TO RING BELLS

Most of the priests I have met in Bali told me that it took them at least a year to learn how to ring a bell correctly. Different buildings call for different kinds of ringing, and the individual rooms within that building may differ widely from one another too. In one room you may feel the need to ring the bell quite vigorously, and the next room may call for a much slower, gentler rhythm. Follow your feelings. In time, if you do enough work with bells, you can learn to read exactly what is happening with the energy of a place by the resonance of a bell.

6. *Shield the space.*

CHECKING THE SPACE IS CLEAR

After doing the Space Clearing, you may like to go around again and check that the energy is now clear. If you find there are still a few places where the energy feels sticky or hot, you need to clap those places out again and rebalance with the bells. Some people cannot feel the energy so easily but can see the transformation that has taken place because the rooms look brighter and clearer. Others notice that their breathing is more free and easy.

If you cannot feel or see any noticeable difference, just assume the Space Clearing has been effective and continue. Your results in the days and weeks ahead will allow you to gauge the effectiveness of the procedures.

BASIC SHIELDING

When you are satisfied that the space is as clear as you are going to be able to get it, this is the time to shield the area so that what you put into the space in the next stage will not leak out. The purpose of this kind of shielding is essentially containment, although it can be used equally well for protection. I have already explained in the last chapter in a different context why I believe shielding for protection is unnecessary (see page 66).

Before you can learn how to shield a whole building, it is easier to learn how to shield an individual room. Pick a room that is square or rectangular, and stand in one corner of the room with your back squarely to the wall. You can use either your right arm or your left arm to do shielding, but just for the sake of explanation, let's say you decide to use your right arm. This means that you will be working around the room in a counterclockwise direction.

With your back square to the wall that you are about to shield, take a breath and raise your arm up above your head with your hand outstretched flat and parallel to the wall. Now release your breath and lower your arm in a wide arc fairly swiftly back down to your side, with your hand still parallel to the wall. As you do, visualize a shield of vibrant light coming out of your fingertips and extending all the way along the wall, covering the whole area. It helps if you make a kind of swishing sound through your teeth as you exhale. The best way I can describe this practice is that it is a bit like the force shields you see on *Star Trek*!

Now walk to the corner you have just extended a shield toward, turn ninety degrees, and drop a shield along the wall to the next corner. Do the same in the other two corners, until you get back to the corner you first started from. You have now shielded all four walls of the room.

To shield the floor, stand at one end of the room roughly in the center of the space and visualize a bright carpet of light unfolding under your feet and extending all the way across the floor to the other side of the room. Now unfurl a similar shield across the entire width and length of the ceiling, completing the shield for the entire room.

Draw the arm down while visualizing a shield

Stand in the middle of the room, fix the visual image of the shields strongly in your mind, and specify how long you want the shields to stay in place. If you want them to be more or less permanent, ask your brain to automatically reinforce the vibrancy of the shields each night before you go to sleep, without your even having to think of it. If you give an instruction to your brain, it will carry on doing it until you instruct it otherwise. If you want the shields to be temporary, instruct your brain to dismantle them at a predetermined time, say, 6 P.M. the next day, or "after Aunt Mabel has gone home, whenever that may be."

SHIELDING IRREGULARLY SHAPED SPACES

There are two different ways to put up shields in rooms that are not exactly square or rectangular. The first way is to ignore the fact that there are chunks missing and drop your shields to extend beyond the physical space of the room to symbolically square it off. This can be very useful in terms of bringing in missing areas of the Feng Shui *bagua*, which is explained later in the book.

Sometimes, however, it may be inappropriate to do the shielding this way. One example would be if you have a missing corner that actually forms part of the apartment next door. Obviously you wouldn't want to bring that into your space by including it in the shielded area. In this circumstance, the best thing to do is to follow the exact contours of the room, which may mean the room has six corners rather than four.

SHIELDING A WHOLE BUILDING

After you have practiced shielding individual rooms and feel satisfied that it is working, you are ready to move on to bigger areas. One way to shield a whole house is to go outside and throw shields into position from one corner to the next as you walk around the outside perimeter of the space. I rarely use this method, however, because I have found I get better results by doing the shielding from inside the house. I have shielded so many spaces that I no longer need to walk from corner to corner to do it. I can just stand by the front door and, in a matter of a few seconds, I visualize shields locking into place on all four walls of the building and the floor and roof. It's a bit like learning to drive a car—you need to go through the basics of it until it all becomes automatic, and then you can do it without having to think about each maneuver.

TAKING SHIELDS DOWN

If at any future time you decide that you want to take these shields down, just visualize them dissolving away. Whenever I put up shields in the course of a Space Clearing consultation in a client's home, I always include the instruction that the shields dissolve if ever the person wishes the work I have done to be undone. This is so that the person can change the energy independently if so desired.

DIFFERENT TYPES OF SHIELDS

The best kind of general purpose shield is one of pure, vibrant light. When I first began putting up shields, I used to practice with a group of friends, and we would experiment with the effects of different colors. We would also play games, such as everyone leaving the room while one person put up a shield, and then the others came back into the room and tried to sense what color the shield was. After a while we got so good at it that we would try to trick each other by erecting combination shields, such as yellow overlaid with blue, or white with pink polka dots! It was a lot of fun, but more importantly it proved to me beyond a shadow of a doubt that putting up these shields wasn't just something in my imagination. When you put up shields in this way, they really do exist, and other people who are sensitive to these things can sense them and see them too.

Use a blue shield for peace and relaxation. For more love, use a beautiful soft pink color. If your focus is on purity, use white. For more vibrancy, use green. For deep healing work, use layers of green and yellow together. Do not use red because it can overstimulate, resulting in friction and arguments.

PERSONAL SHIELDING

Although shielding yourself is unnecessary for Space Clearing work (if you feel fear then you shouldn't proceed with Space Clearing anyway), you may sometimes come across situations in your life when you feel fearful and would like to use a personal shield to create your own sacred space inside your aura. You can do this by using a similar technique to the one I have just described for buildings. It's best to practice a bit so that you feel confident to use the technique when you really feel you need it.

Just visualize the edge of your aura encapsulated in a bubble. That's it! You are now shielded. You can use a bubble of pure vibrant light or the different colors described above according to requirement. If you are very afraid, put up a black shield for maximum protection but remember to take it down again once the danger has passed, because otherwise people will start saying to you, "I feel like I'm not getting through to you," or "I feel like you're not really here." Again, you can specify a time when the shield is to come down, or a situation (say, when you are safely back inside your home).

If you do use shields, intend to use them less and less as time goes by and your confidence increases. The best protection of all is to surround yourself with the radiation of love.

7. Fill the space with intention, light, and love.

Having cleared your home of all the things you no longer want and shielded it to maintain the new purity of the space, the natural thing to do next is to fill it up with something better. After Space Clearing you have a clean sheet, a fresh start, and what you do next is very important. If you don't make conscious decisions about what to fill the space with, you will just start to collect more of the same stuff you have just dispersed.

There are many types and levels of dedication, depending on how much time and energy you want to put into the process. First sit quietly and read through the description of your ideal life that you wrote in the preparation stage (see Step 5 of Preparation). Focus your attention as fully as you can.

USING HARMONY BALLS

The best way I have found of doing the next bit is to use harmony balls. These are metal balls that make lovely soft chiming sounds when you shake them. The Chinese use similar chrome-plated pairs of balls for healing purposes, and they are designed to be held in your hand and rotated around each other. Mayan chime balls from South America are lighter in weight and more suitable for Space Clearing purposes. The ones I use are from Bali, are made of brass, and are about one and one-half inches in diameter.

Sit quietly, close your eyes, and cup a harmony ball between your hands. Let your breathing become deep and regular and focus your attention on your heart. Allow the love from your heart to expand out to fill your body, passing down your arms, through your hands, and into the harmony ball. Fill the harmony ball with love.

Now focus your attention on the center of the harmony ball. Image into it everything that you want to have happen in your life from now on. If you are the head of the household and are acting on behalf of others, include the wish that all their deepest, most heartfelt desires be fulfilled. Do it deep and do it strong. Make the images as real and colorful as you can. Bring them to life with sounds, smells, tastes, and textures. Be sure to include pictures of yourself and those you love looking radiantly happy, healthy, and successful. Know that your most heartfelt desires are beacons from your higher self to lead you to the purpose you came here to fulfill. If you are not sure exactly what you want, visualize more clarity coming into your life. Conclude by mentally saying: "May this or something better now manifest for the highest good of all concerned."

Now take the harmony ball and, starting at the front entrance, go around the inside perimeter of your space one final time, shaking what you have imaged into the ball into the atmosphere of your home. It is important to keep up a good pace as you do this so that the energy is as full and vibrant as possible. You may add other harmony balls to give a fuller sound (I usually use three). The Balinese ones have a wonderful, jingly-jangly magical sound, as if there are a thousand fairies on the job!

As you go around each room, visualize it filling with beautiful cascading light coming from the harmony balls, and breathe deeply, filling your lungs with your new life. By the time you get back to the front entrance, your home will be full of your wonderful new future.

I have found it to be far more effective to use visualization in conjunction with harmony balls because you have the physical experience of actually going from room to room and putting the new energy into the atmosphere. If you have children, give them each a ball and get them to come and help you do it. They love it!

If you don't have a harmony ball, a good alternative would be a small tinkly bell. Or just use your own hands—cup them together during the visualization to build up an energy ball between them and then swirl the essence of it out into the space with your hands.

I have been asked a few times whether it is possible to do Space Clearing entirely by visualization. You certainly can visualize doing Space Clearing and send the energy ahead of you into the future to enhance its effectiveness when you do it, but it is not a substitute for physically rolling up your sleeves and doing it.

S P A C E   C L E A R I N G   T I P S

A night in Calcutta

One of my most memorable Space Clearing experiences happened during my backpacking days, when I stayed overnight in Calcutta in a hotel room that I discovered was littered with enormous dead cockroaches. I will always remember sitting gingerly on the edge of my bed, my skin crawling at the thought of having cockroaches scuttling over me while I slept. Suddenly it came to me! Cockroaches inhabit the lowest level of astral light. That's why they are so repulsive. I realized I could Space Clear the room and raise the level of the astral light so that they wouldn't be attracted into my space. I got out of bed, lit lots of incense, Space Cleared the entire room, zapped the energy up a few levels, shielded the space, and got back into bed. I still slept with one eye open, but it was an uneventful night with not a cockroach in sight.

"Maybe there weren't any live cockroaches in the place anyway," I thought in the morning as I opened the door to leave and surveyed the empty corridor. Then, being an orderly kind of person, I took down the shield I had put up and suddenly, from nowhere, a swarm of cockroaches appeared and rushed between my feet into the room as I picked up my bags and rushed out!

I have since used this technique in many different tropical countries known to have cockroaches and have never been troubled by them again. When I stayed with friends in Australia recently, they were amazed that the cockroaches disappeared for the two weeks I was there and reappeared again after I had left. Space Clearing did the trick!

Space Clearing for travelers

I had some incense with me on that memorable night in Calcutta, but I certainly didn't have a bell or any of the other equipment that I normally use for Space Clearing. What I did have was a very strong intention and the ability to improvise. If you travel a lot you might like to put together a small travel kit for Space Clearing, which would include some incense, a candle, matches, a small bottle of holy water, a small quantity of salt in a sealed container, and a tiny bell. You can use any fresh flowers, fruit, other food, or a few coins of the local currency as an offering.

Giving your home a regular check-up

The first time you do Space Clearing in your home is similar to doing a very thorough spring cleaning. Do it as deeply and powerfully as possible to leave your home feeling clear, vibrant, and energized. This will diminish with time as stuck energy starts to accumulate again, and so you need to check at regular intervals to see how much buildup there is.

Some houses and people build up stuck energy quicker than others. This depends on the Feng Shui of your home, what is happening in your life, what kind of person you are, and so on. For most people I suggest that every month or two after doing the initial major Space Clearing ceremony, you repeat the exercises to sensitize your hands and then go around the inside perimeter of the walls again, sensing how the energy feels.

You can do the entire basic Space Clearing ceremony every week if you choose to, but this really isn't necessary. For most people, once or twice a year is enough, unless you have specific energy you need to clear or many major changes happening in your life. To maintain high-quality atmospheres in your home in between major clearings, you can do maintenance Space Clearing once a month and refresh your atmospheres once a week after doing your physical cleaning.

Maintenance Space Clearing

For this you will need a candlelit flower offering, a leaf, some incense and an incense holder, some matches, a bell, and some holy water. Place the candlelit offering and incense in the power center of your home (this may not be the exact center but a place from where you feel you can access the entire energy of your space), remembering to place a leaf underneath the saucer. Put the incense stick next to it in an incense holder, light the incense and the candle, and sprinkle holy water on the offering. As you do so, focus your intention for the ceremony and connect with the energy of your home. Offer prayers and call in helpers from the unseen realms if you wish to.

Starting at the front door, go around the entire inner perimeter of the space, clapping in all the corners, and then go around a second time ringing the bell to produce a sacred circle of sound. Then renew your shields and visualize the whole space full of vibrant energy.

Refreshing your atmospheres

You can refresh your atmospheres as you need to by using quick and effective techniques such as spraying a mixture of water and lavender oil into the air or playing beautiful music. Choose from the range of techniques described in Part Two of this book.

Important note

The Space Clearing techniques in this book are designed only for personal use. A whole bank of additional information and training is necessary for anyone wishing to do Space Clearing professionally in order to learn how to handle the huge amounts of energy involved. People are very connected to their homes, and when you do Space Clearing you are dealing on a very, very intimate and personal level with the energy of those people's lives. Without specific training, you are likely to make unfortunate blunders. Quite aside from the karmic implications of messing up other people's lives, you also run the risk of harming your own health and well-being. Please use this information responsibly.

BASIC SPACE CLEARING
CHECKLIST

Preparation

1. Do not attempt Space Clearing if you feel any fear or apprehension. These techniques are perfectly safe but are designed
   for personal everyday use, not for the purposes of exorcism—
   leave that to trained professionals.
2. Obtain permission before doing Space Clearing in someone
   else's personal space.
3. Do Space Clearing when you feel physically fit and healthy,
   emotionally centered, and mentally focused.
4. It is best not to do Space Clearing if you are pregnant, menstruating, or have an open flesh wound.
5. Take the time to think about what you want to have happen
   in your life. If you share the space with others, it is best to
   consult them too.
6. For best results, physically clean and straighten up the space,
   sweep, mop or vacuum it, and clear out clutter first.
7. Take a full bath or shower, or at least wash your face and
   hands.
8. Put food and drink away in cupboards or sealed containers.
9. Remove jewelry and other metallic objects from your person.
   Work barefoot if possible.
10. Work alone unless other people present fully understand what
    you are doing.

11. Work in silence without background music. Turn off any fans and other nonessential loud or droning machinery.
12. Open a door or a window.
13. Locate an appropriate power point and set up your Space Clearing equipment.
14. Roll up your sleeves and sensitize your hands.

Procedures

1. Take time to attune to the space. Mentally announce yourself and radiate your intention.
2. Starting at the main entrance, go around the inside perimeter of the space, sensing the energy. Use your hands and all your other senses too.
3. Light candles, burn incense, sprinkle holy water, and offer flowers and prayers to the guardian spirit of the house and the spirits of earth, air, fire, and water. Call in the angels and your own personal guides and helpers (whatever feels appropriate to you).
4. Clap in corners to disperse static energy. Then wash your hands in running water (very important to remember to do this).
5. Purify the space with bells.
6. Shield the space.
7. Fill the space with intention, light, and love.

PART TWO

Methods of Purification

8.

Purification by Sound

This section of the book looks at each of the different methods of purification through sound and the four elements of earth, air, fire, and water. It includes more detailed information about basic Space Clearing techniques, together with information about other Space Clearing techniques you might like to add to or substitute for basic procedures outlined in Part One as you become more experienced. You will also learn how to adapt Space Clearing techniques for personal usage to clear your own energy field.

CLAPPING

The most powerful Space Clearing techniques I know are those using the vibration of sound, which can penetrate any substance and produce profound shifts in energy very quickly. All I had done at the point when Denise Linn walked into that room in the anecdote she recounts in the foreword to this book is a specific kind of clapping technique. It is so simple and yet so powerfully effective. It works because the sound vibrations break up congealed lumps of energy.

The ancient Chinese knew about clapping. Chinese theater and dance were designed not as entertainment for the masses as Western theater is today but to invoke the presence of the gods. Those who went to watch would never clap at the end of the performance but would leave in silence because they wanted to take the essence of what they had witnessed home with them. They would, however, clap at the beginning to clear the space.

In Japan they have a Space Clearing ceremony in which they use the point of a sword to disperse static energy that collects in the corners of rooms. I've tried using a sword and also a wooden pointed stick. They both work reasonably well, and if you send energy out from your hand down the sword or stick with the intention of dispersing the static, it is even more effective. For elderly or physically disabled people who have difficulty clapping, a sword or a pointed stick is a very viable alternative to clapping, but I have found clapping to be more thorough, and it has the added advantage of not needing any equipment. I dare say I would be arrested in some parts of the world if I traveled from consultation to consultation with a Japanese sword slung across my back!

Some people who have been to my workshops have put clapping to ingenious uses. One man had a car that was always breaking down. On his own initiative he decided one day to clap out the interior of the car, and many months later he reported to me that it had been completely trouble-free ever since. "You've saved me a fortune in repair bills!" he added.

To refresh your own energy, clap out your own aura for half a minute or so, especially the areas around the feet and around the head. You can do it yourself or have a friend do it for you. If ever you feel "spaced out," one of the quickest, safest, and most effective ways I know of bringing yourself back down to earth is a few loud, crisp claps into each ear.

DRUMMING

All shamanic work is based on the rhythm of the drum. Bali is famous for its xylophone-like gamelan orchestras, which consist of two drummers leading between twenty-five and fifty musicians. The head drummer is the most respected player in any gamelan orchestra, since he must also be a master of every other instrument in the orchestra.

In terms of Space Clearing work, drums can be used very effectively in the same way as clapping, and Denise Linn has developed the art to a very high level. In her book, *Sacred Space*, she gives detailed information about using drums in this way.

ASSORTED PERCUSSION AND SQUEAKERS

Over the years, I have built up a huge collection of percussive objects, which can be used in different ways in Space Clearing work, such as clap sticks (two sticks that you bang together), rattles, shakers, and squeakers. The most amusing of these—and one that always gets a laugh at my workshops—is a small plastic squeaker, which I found in a breakfast cereal packet many years ago and which sounds like an indignant cartoon character. It is the best antidote I have ever found for dispersing the aftereffects of an argument in a room. You can sometimes find similar squeakers for sale in notions stores.

BELLS

The vibration of a good quality bell will disperse levels of stuck energy, which clapping cannot dislodge, and create a sacred circle of sound that will reverberate in your atmospheres for a long time. People often tell me that months after I have been to Space Clear their homes, they still sometimes hear the shimmering sounds of the bells! The traditional Christian practice of ringing church bells in the parish on a Sunday morning is an example of Space Clearing on a grand scale! I believe those who started the practice knew exactly what they were doing in this respect.

I love bells and have been collecting them from all over the world for over twenty years. When I first began learning how to Space Clear, I used any bell I could get my hands on, but now I am what you might call a bell connoisseur.

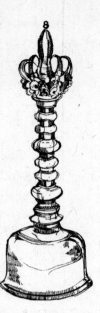

Balinese temple bell

My Balinese temple bell

This is such a wonderful story and such a milestone in my Space Clearing work that I feel it is worth telling in full. I had been in Bali for exactly three weeks when I was invited to a cremation ceremony in a remote, very poor Balinese village. The ceremony was fascinating—a joyous, colorful, dramatic event attended by hundreds of people clad in their best sarongs, culminating in setting fire to the ornate, funerary tower in a small clearing near the temple.

In the distance I could hear being rung from time to time a bell that had the purest sound I had ever heard. I had to know what it was. I made my way through the crowds and discovered a priestess sitting on a small table, dressed entirely in white. Surrounding her on the table were heaps of offerings of freshly picked flower petals and fruits in decorative palm leaf baskets, interlaced with sticks of smoking incense. In front of her was a silver vessel containing holy water, which she flicked with a bundle of sacred grasses onto the offerings placed in front of her as she chanted various mantras.

As I neared the spot, she put down the grasses, picked up a beautiful bell in her left hand, and began to ring a continuous ding-a-ling-a-ling as she chanted more mantras and performed a graceful series of actions with flower petals and holy water with her right hand. I turned to the Balinese friend who had brought me to the ceremony and said, "I really want a bell like that. Where can I get one?" He smiled a proud smile, pleased that I was so impressed with the bell, but said as kindly as possible that I should forget all about wanting to own such a bell because they are only ever made for Balinese priests and priestesses.

In the days that followed I checked among other Balinese friends and they all assured me that there was no possibility of a westerner ever being able to own such a bell. No one could even tell me where they were made. They spoke with reverence of the magical powers of the bells, which only deepened my desire to have one!

I went into a process of prayer and affirmation and continued to ask everyone I met if they might be able to help me. This went on for the better part of a year. Finally, miraculously, I met a priest who understood exactly why I wanted a bell and was willing to help me. He directed me to a place that was a day's journey from where I was staying, involving eight changes of buses there and back, but I didn't care. I was prepared to make the journey as many times as necessary, and probably because of this willingness, I didn't have to. I met someone who took me to meet the family of bell-makers right away.

After this began a series of visits to the family, spanning a period of another year. I was getting to know them, and they were getting to know me. We talked about bells and about my Space Clearing work in the West. I learned that all the best metalworkers in Bali belong to a highly respected special caste called the *Pandé*. They told me that the priests' bells have brass handles, and the domes are made of bronze mixed with twenty-two carat gold, which is partly what gives them the superb purity of tone. The rest is a result of the skill of the crafting process, which has been handed down through generations.

I discovered that the production process is always begun at the full moon, which is the most potent time of the moon's cycle. Each bell takes two months to make, and offerings are made to the Balinese gods at each stage of the production process to ensure its purity. Immense care is always taken to ensure that each and every bell is of the highest quality. When a priest or priestess receives a new bell, they will not use it in their work until they have performed an elaborate consecration ceremony to bring it to life. The ceremony takes place in their temple on an auspicious day determined according to the Balinese calendar system.

The quality of the crafting is such that a Balinese temple bell can be put to rigorous use on a daily basis by the priest or priestess and his or her descendants for perhaps a hundred years or more. The cost of the materials to make the bell, the skilled work to produce it, and the ceremonial offerings to sanctify it mean that it may well take the resources of an entire village to fund a replacement bell when necessary.

When I felt the time was right, I asked them if they would be willing to make me one of these bells to use in my work and, to my delight, they agreed. It cost a fortune but I was happy to pay it. The priest who had first put me on the path of finding the bell-maker's family performed the consecration ceremony for me, and I have used it virtually every day since then. It does the work of all the other bells I used to use, and more. I call it affectionately "The Mother of All Bells"!

That was in 1992. I brought it back to England and began to use it in my Space Clearing work and public workshops. In 1993 there was an explosion of interest in people wanting to learn about Feng Shui and Space Clearing. After attending my workshops, more and more people started asking me where they could buy a good quality bell so that they could put into practice what they had learned. I scoured the country but found no manufacturers of suitable bells at all, and at that time all I could suggest was that they look in junk shops and oriental musical instrument shops.

Balinese Space Clearing bells

This dilemma continued for several years. It felt awkward for me to teach Space Clearing workshops and not be able to offer people the tools to go and begin using the information in their own homes, but there was nothing I could recommend they use. The bell-makers could only craft a handful of temple bells a year and these were very expensive and all needed for Balinese priests and priestesses.

Gradually two things became very obvious to me: Firstly, there are no other bells in the world to compare with Balinese bells.[1] And secondly, for people to be completely safe doing Space Clearing, they must use a Balinese bell rather than any other type. I hadn't realized this when I first began teaching the material but I now know it's an absolute must.

In 1995, I discussed the problem with the bell-makers. I asked them if they would make a simpler version of a temple bell with the same excellent purity of sound but a smaller dome and a wooden handle instead of a brass one. This was a design we worked out together specifically for Space Clearing work in the West and suitable for all the levels of Space Clearing described in this book. I am happy to say they are now producing these high-quality bells in quantity and they are available to anyone.

The next development was in 1997. Most people were delighted with the Space Clearing bell but for larger buildings and more advanced chakra balancing work, it was clear a larger bell was required. And thus the Empress bell was born! Though I say it myself, it's beautiful! The dome of this bell is the same size as the original Balinese temple bell but it has a beautifully carved wooden handle instead. By 1999, all the technical difficulties had been overcome and it became possible to also handcraft these bells in quantity.

Space Clearing and Empress bells are available from my website, my U.K. and U.S. Offices, and also from the shop at my hotel in Bali (see Resources at the back of this book). They can both be used for Space Clearing and the chakra balancing work described later in this chapter.

[1] I exclude from this the shoddily-made imitation temple bells you can now find in some Balinese markets and shops, made by unscrupulous entrepreneurs cashing in on the demand created by the popularity of this book. It's an embarrassment to me that this has happened but there is nothing I can do except warn you about it and let you know you would be wasting your money.

Caring for bells

If you have a bell that is special to you, create a special place to keep it when not in use. In keeping with Balinese tradition, I keep mine in an elevated position, away from where anyone habitually lies or sleeps with their feet pointing in that direction. It is a matter of personal choice whether you let others handle your bell or not. However, if it is important to you to maintain the purity of its vibration, I recommend that you be selective about who touches it and why. I now have one Balinese temple bell that I use in my public work and that others'may touch if invited, and another identical bell that only my partner and I ever touch. I have definitely noticed a difference in energies between the two bells.

If you tune in, your bell will let you know what it needs and how best to use it. I remember the first time I brought my bell back from Bali, I met up with Sean Milligan, a conscious and very talented percussionist. He had never been to Bali, but to my total astonishment, he picked up the bell and began to ring it *exactly* the same way that an experienced Balinese priest would. When I asked him how he knew how to ring it, he simply shrugged his shoulders and said, "The bell told me!"

Chakra balancing with bells

Something I often do in my workshops to show how bells work is to demonstrate chakra balancing. I have someone sit upright in a straight-backed chair with their legs and arms uncrossed and their hands resting loosely in their lap and not touching each other. When they are comfortable I explain what I am about to do and let them know that they can either have their eyes open or closed, whichever feels best to them. I stand next to them, angling my body at forty-five degrees to theirs, so that it is as if I am nudging into their aura elbow first rather than confronting them head-on.

I position the bell about six inches in front of them at the level of their base chakra. Next I tell them to take a deep breath, as if they were breathing all the way down to their toes and back out again. While they are doing this, I synchronize my breathing with theirs and then tell them to continue breathing normally. At the bottom of the outbreath I ring the bell and slowly move it up the central meridian of their body, keeping a distance of about six inches away from them, following the contours of their profile. I bring the bell up past their solar plexus, heart, throat, forehead, and right up to the top of the head and twelve inches or so higher. Then, to complete the movement, I twist the bell a half-turn to lock in the results of what I have done so that the beneficial effects last longer.

Often I do two or three passes of the bell like this, each time synchronizing the breathing before I begin and letting the person know what I am about to do. I very rarely come across anyone who needs more than three passes of the bell to bring themselves into alignment.

This chakra balancing is something I usually offer now to people after I have finished going around their house with the bells, and it allows me to work on a very deep and intimate level with them. From working in this way I obtain an incredible amount of information about the person, and it is always reliable. When I used to work as a bodyworker, I often used to say, "The body never lies." Now, in this kind of work I say, "The bell never lies."

When I do chakra balancing in front of a group of people at a workshop, I often get half a dozen people to come and sit facing the group, and I work along the row one by one. Always by the second or third person there are gasps of amazement from the audience as they realize that every person sounds completely different. The bell fades in and out according to the balance of a person's chakras. If a person is in good shape, the bell sounds absolutely clear and resonant all the way up, but if there are areas that need attention, the sound drops and then fades in again, often changing several times between base and crown chakra. By the second or third pass the difference is remarkable. The sound becomes—to coin a phrase—as clear as a bell! Another interesting feature is that when I do this in front of a whole group of people, each person watching feels an empathy with at least one of the people I have picked to demonstrate on, and they tell me it is as if they all receive the same result by proxy.

You can also balance your own chakras with a bell using exactly the same technique. You can do this sitting or standing, as you prefer. Only use bells of the highest quality for this type of work because otherwise you can cause more harm than good.

The most moving experience I ever had with my bell involved a small boy who was so shy that he ran away and hid under the table when I arrived to do Space Clearing in his parents' home. As I unpacked my bag full of beautiful brass and silver equipment and began my work, his curiosity got the better of him, and by the time we got to the stage of working with the harmony balls, he had become my assistant. We went around the house together, and he did all the places under tables and desks, while I looked after the upper areas.

At the end of the session, I offered to do chakra balancing with my bell. First I did the father, then the mother, and then I looked at the little boy. "Do you want a chance?" I asked him, and he nodded and climbed up into the chair. As soon as I had finished he climbed off the chair and disappeared upstairs to his bedroom without a word, reappearing a few seconds later with his most prized possession, his security blanket. To my amazement, he dropped it on the chair and looked at me appealingly. He wanted me to chakra balance his blanket! Well, I had never done a blanket before, but I balanced it and I balanced it good! It was an honor, a privilege, and a very touching experience.

Balancing energy in rooms with bells

In my Space Clearing work these days, I generally go once around with my Balinese temple bell to clear energies and create a sacred circle of sound, and then I go around the space again using a Balinese Space Clearing bell together with my temple bell to balance the energies. The interval between the two bells is such that their tones resonate in sympathetic harmony and resound magically throughout the space. It is as if the whole place is alive and singing! This delicate tuning of the atmospheres is something that can only be learned by the experience of doing it in many different spaces.

CYMBALS

You can use these for Space Clearing, but the technique is a little different. You ding the two small cymbals together, and then sweep them up and down as you walk around the space, bathing the walls continually with sound. Finish at the same place you started, and then go into the center of the room and use the two cymbals to balance the energy of the space.

SINGING BOWLS

These can be used for Space Clearing, but I have found them to be not as effective as bells. Their bowl shape is much more feminine in nature than an upright bell, and therefore more receptive in nature than active. They are also more cumbersome to carry around than bells. Singing bowls are excellent, however, for inducting beautiful fine atmospheres after a space has been cleared, and they really come into their own when you use them in the same way as you would use a bell for chakra balancing.

GONGS

These are even less portable than singing bowls but very effective for Space Clearing. Gongs are deep and powerful and ancient. If you place one in an accessible position in a building, very few people can resist the urge to strike it as they pass.

The sound of a large gong resonates into every part of a space (including you!) and is immensely purifying and energizing. Balinese gamelan orchestras consist of many varieties of gongs and metal xylophone instruments and generate an incredible evocative syncopation of sound to summon the gods to temple ceremonies.

WIND CHIMES

The delicate sounds of wind chimes are of minor use in Space Clearing ceremonials but very useful to maintain the purity of an atmosphere on a daily basis. In the United States it is possible to buy electronic wind chimes that can be programmed when you wake up in the morning for anything from a gentle breeze to a full-blown tornado! They are best used in conjunction with Feng Shui placement principles (see Chapter 19).

MUSIC

Music is an excellent means of inducting different atmospheres and refreshing existing ones. Start to become more conscious of the music that you listen to and the effect it has on you, especially music with sung lyrics. Language has a powerful effect on the subconscious mind, and negative lyrics listened to again and again will create negative programming in your mind.

CHANTING AND SINGING

Using your own voice is a very exciting way of working with sound, because the energy comes directly through you. The human voice has the potential to be more powerful than any musical instrument on earth.

Many people find chanting is the easiest way to begin. You find a mantra that feels meaningful to you, and you chant it over and over, again and again. Many mantras are in Sanskrit, the oldest language in the world. Hari Sharma says about it in his book, *Freedom from Disease*, "The language was not invented but cognized by enlightened sages who could hear subtle fluctuations in the fields of intelligence around them." The vibrations of the words themselves bring about changes in you and in the atmosphere of the room, even if you do not know what they mean. You can use chanting to invoke new atmospheres or refresh existing ones.

Singing will also very effectively lift an atmosphere. Have you ever tried singing when you feel depressed? It's the last thing you feel like doing! But when you are happy and you sing from your heart, you fill the space with joy!

TONING

Toning does not have the structure of chanting but has the potential to be immensely powerful. I believe it will be used more and more in the years to come, not only for Space Clearing but also for powerful healing work and as a method of accessing information that we need for our future development.

Toning comes from deep inside you. If the situation you are reading this book in is appropriate, just take a breath, open your mouth, and make a sound *right now*. Let it come out of you loudly and powerfully and naturally. By varying the shape of the cavity of your mouth and moving your lips, you can hold the note yet vary the sound tremendously. This is you toning you.

To tone to Space Clear a room you first of all have to connect with the room and then make whatever sound is needed to do the job. You go to the walls and tone deeply into them, using the vibration of your own voice to do what you would with bells.

You can also tone to clear an object. Bring your mouth up close to it and tone powerfully into it. If it is a large object, you will need to move your head so that you tone into every part of it. If it is a small object, it works very well to cup it in your hands as you tone.

9.

Purification by Earth, Water, Air, and Fire

Feng Shui is about living in harmony with our environment, with the four primary elements of earth, air, fire, and water. Traditional cultures are very conscious of the awesome power of these elements and seek to invoke the blessings of the sylphs of the air, the undines of water, the gnomes of the earth and the salamanders of fire, all known by different names in different parts of the world. These invisible planetary life-forms find the coarse, hot vibration of the electricity we use to power our machines very difficult to be with for long, and yet they love to be with us if they can.

One of the reasons why so much preparation is necessary for Space Clearing work is to create as inviting an environment as possible to attract the presence of these representatives of the fairy worlds. Each type of nature spirit works in its own element, and this chapter of the book offers more in-depth information about the different methods of purification they can work through.

Note that purification through the four natural elements is not to be confused with the classical Chinese five-element theory, based on cyclic progressions, which is used in other branches of Feng Shui for divinatory purposes.

P U R I F I C A T I O N   B Y   E A R T H

In some temples of the world visitors are required to remove their shoes before entering, partly to leave lower, impure energies outside and partly so that the potent earth energies of that place can enter through their feet and fill their bodies. Some deep instinct draws us to make pilgrimages to these sacred sites, to connect with the ancient healing power of the earth and knowledge stored in sacred places. No purification ceremony would be complete wihtout representing elements of Mother Earth.

Flowers

In the West men give flowers to their sweethearts, but in Bali they give flowers only to the gods! Late afternoon vendors open on street corners all over the island to sell heaps of freshly picked flower heads in decorative coconut leaf baskets, which are used to make offerings in household shrines and temples. They are offering back to the earth the highest part of herself.

Flowers form an integral part of all Space Clearing and consecration ceremonies, and much information has already been given in earlier chapters. Always use fresh flowers and, if possible, pick them yourself from a living plant. Remember to ask permission from the plant before doing so.

In everyday living, the aromas, colors, and subtle emanations of flowers all contribute to the effect they can have on a space. A beautiful bunch of cut flowers or a pretty flowering plant will refine and brighten any atmosphere.

Stones

One very easy way to anchor energy after you have Space Cleared is to position stones in each of the corners of the space. I generally prefer to use rounded stones, such as you might find washed up on a beach or in a river. You visualize the stones fixing the energy in place (very much as you might use stones to weigh down the canopy of a tent so that it won't blow away in the wind).

Sequins

A variation on stones is large sequins, which are more rarefied and also more transportable. If I feel the need, I sometimes put sequins in the corners of a room in which I am teaching a workshop. They hold the energy and maintain its level. The sequins I use are about one inch in diameter and come in various colors. I may use different colors in each corner for a varied effect, or the same color all around for a specific frequency.

Salt

There is enough salt in the oceans of the world to cover all the continents with a layer almost five hundred feet thick. Every culture in the world uses it as a powerful agent of purification. In Europe, it used to be a common practice to sprinkle a pinch of salt out of the front door before everyone went to bed at night to ensure safety during sleep. In some parts of Egypt, all the floors of a house are covered with salt at the beginning of the month of Ramadan, when Muslims purify themselves by fasting from sunrise to sunset. Sumo wrestlers throw salt to purify the space energetically before they engage physically with one another. In the English language we talk about someone being "worth their salt," meaning they are efficient and capable, and we call someone of great worthiness "the salt of the earth."

In natural healing practices, salt is held in equally high esteem because of its powerful antiseptic properties. One naturopath has devised a remarkable system of healing to cure every known ailment, and it is based on using just four items that are naturally available everywhere: lemons, garlic, ice, and salt.

The best salt to use for Space Clearing is unrefined sea salt or rock salt, and it must be kept in a sealed container until you want to use it. As soon as salt is exposed to the air, it starts to absorb impurities from the surrounding atmosphere.

I love the feel of salt in my hands, and I use it in many different ways. To enhance basic Space Clearing procedures, I begin by putting a line of salt across every threshold, paying particular attention to the main front entrance. After this I go around the space and do the clapping and other procedures. For deeper cleansing I will also put salt in every corner and in the middle of every room (it can be put in small bowls if preferred). For very, very deep cleansings I throw salt everywhere.

It is best left in place for about twenty-four hours, and then it can be swept or vacuumed up and thrown away. The bowls of salt also need to be left for twenty-four hours, and if you have cleared a lot of stuck energy, it is sometimes beneficial to renew the salt in the bowls every day for a week or so. The best way to dispose of salt is to take it to the ocean or to the nearest river if you conveniently live near one; if you live inland, just tip it down the toilet. Under no circumstances should it be used for cooking after it has been used for Space Clearing!

If you have a room in your home that you use for healing or meditation, you may like to keep a bowl of salt in there all the time, but do remember to refresh it every day. Salt can lower the vibration of a space rather than raise it once it has become saturated with impurities. You can also put a bowl of salt next to your bed or put a circle of salt around your bed to improve the quality of your sleep.

Crystals

The type of crystals used for earth purification are unpolished minerals mined from the earth rather than the manufactured leaded rainbow crystals (designed to simulate flawless cut diamonds) generally used for Feng Shui cures and enhancements (see Chapter 19).

You can program crystals to anchor and purify energy to help you maintain high-quality atmospheres in your home. First you will need to cleanse your crystal by washing it in holy water or charged water (see page

136) made without using salt (salt can cause microscopic damage to crystals). Another method is to bury the crystal in sea salt or bury it in the earth for a period of time (some time between an hour and a day is usually sufficient). You can also visualize pure vibrant white light cleansing the crystal, you can tone into it, and you can use your breath to blow out old frequencies. Use whichever method works best for you.

To program a crystal you need to connect with its frequency. Talk to it simply, respectfully, firmly, and kindly. Hold it in your hands and say to it, "Your job is . . . ." The crystal will then do this forever unless you tell it to stop. Another way to program a crystal is to image into it what you want it to do. Or you can hold the crystal to your heart and put the feelings from your heart into the crystal. I use all three methods in combination.

When using crystals it is important to understand that, like jewelry, they were never meant to be used purely for decoration. Avoid having lots of crystals on display near each other, and especially not mixed together in a bowl like an assortment of candy! Whenever I see this in people's homes, I know that there is confusion in their lives. Crystals have their own specific frequencies and need their own space.

If you are not using a crystal, just putting it away in a drawer will not deactivate it. You need to wrap it in aluminum foil (the mirrored surface reflects the energy back to the crystal), and to preserve the purity of each crystal's frequency, wrap only crystals of the same kind together.

PURIFICATION BY WATER

Water is a wonderful natural cleansing agent, and there is a great tradition on our planet of making pilgrimages to sacred springs to "take the waters" for healing purposes. I once went to live for a year next to the Holy Well in Malvern, Worcestershire, in England, because I was doing some very specific purification work and wanted to be close enough to walk to the well and take the waters each day fresh from the water spout. This is spring water freshly made in the bowels of the earth, and it feels and tastes incredible. Malvern water is famous for having absolutely nothing in it except water, and the Queen of England is reputed to drink it everywhere she goes. I had a most remarkable year and learned a lot about the incredible purifying power of water.

Sources of purifying water

For Space Clearing, it is best to use water from a natural spring. Water from a natural waterfall is another excellent source, and water from unpolluted rivers and streams (if you can find them!) is also good. Lake water is not so effective for cleansing purposes generally because its nature is more holding and retentive than cleansing. Distilled water and carbonated spring water are also not recommended.

Holy water in Bali

No ceremony in Bali would be complete without holy water, and making it has been developed to such a high art that there is a different type of holy water for every conceivable purpose. One kind of holy water is used to cleanse the body of sickness, another kind to cleanse the mind of negative thoughts, another kind to cleanse and consecrate buildings, and so on. In his book, *Bali: Sekala and Niskala*, Fred B. Eiseman Jr. explains:

> There are many kinds and potencies of holy water, which vary according to how it is made, its source, and who makes it. The more powerful the mantras used to make it, the more mystic energy it contains. The more sacred the place from which it is obtained, the greater the sanctity of the holy water. The more exalted the status of the person who makes it, the greater its magical power.

He goes on to say,

> Holy water requires special handling and must be treated with respect and deference. The most powerful holy water from the most sacred source, prepared with the most magical mantras by the

most exalted priest, loses its power if treated casually or disrespectfully. On the other hand, clean water from the well of a house compound, placed in a new container in the house of an ordinary family temple becomes powerful and effective holy water if the feelings of the user towards it are properly reverent.

How to make your own holy water

Holy water can be obtained from a priest if you practice a religion that uses it, or you may choose to make your own. One way to do this is to first of all create a special place to hold the ceremony, which can be a permanent altar or a table set up temporarily with a cloth over it. Next take two bowls that have never been used for any other purpose except purification ceremonials and put salt in one bowl and water in the other. The salt needs to have been kept in a sealed container prior to use, and the water needs to be fresh, noncarbonated water, either straight from a natural source or from a newly opened bottle.

Light candles and burn a high-quality incense so that the small area you are working in is filled with its aroma. Ring a bell over the bowls of salt and water to purify the contents. Then with the candles and incense still burning close by, calm your thoughts and hold a hand over each bowl, just above but not touching the salt or the water. Stretch your fingers so that your fingertips point downward toward the bowls. It doesn't matter which way around you have the bowls. Imagine that you are a clear channel for pure, vibrant universal light to come in through the crown chakra at the top of your head and then out through your hands and into the salt and water. You may be able to feel the energy streaming out of your fingertips.

After a while, cross your hands over and continue to let energy pour through you. In this way, both bowls will receive energy from both your left and your right hands. Do this for a few minutes then ring the bell again, and while the sound is still reverberating, take a pinch of salt and drop it into the water, quickly followed by two more pinches of salt, making three in all (you can add more or less salt than this, as you wish). Put the bowl of salt to one side and focus your attention on the bowl containing both the salt and water. Now use both hands together to energize this, until you feel the energy bouncing back to you (a few minutes is usually sufficient). You can add verbal mantras if you know any that are appropriate and mudras (mantras made with sacred gestures of the hands) if you know any of these.

This is the way I usually make holy water. Other ways are to energize it in sunlight or in moonlight or to stand it in a sacred place for a period of time. Combine all methods or use whichever method feels best to you.

Storing holy water

Holy water can be made without salt, but it really helps the water to keep its energy charge longer. It is most potent if you use it immediately, but if you plan to store it, put it in a clean container that has never been used for any other purpose, cap it, and keep it in a special place. This could be on your altar if you have one or somewhere in your home that you feel is special. As a mark of respect, the Balinese always keep their holy water in an elevated position, which helps to maintain its purity.

Using holy water

It is a wonderful practice to take some holy water for yourself each day. You can sprinkle it on your head, put some in the center of your forehead, your temples, throat, the palms of your hands, the soles of your feet, and any parts of your body that need healing or revitalizing. After Space Clearing you can sprinkle holy water around your home, especially across thresholds and in corners. Use a flower head to flick the water. It makes your home feel incredibly clean and fresh and sanctified. Put a bowl of charged salt and water under the bed of anyone who is ill to help the person keep his or her strength up and refresh it daily in the morning. This practice is also useful for children who have nightmares.

Cleansing objects with holy water

You can use holy water to cleanse objects such as jewelry and second-hand items that are washable. Simply wash the object with holy water and allow it to dry naturally. If getting the object wet would damage it, see the information about toning in Chapter 8. To cleanse natural crystals, use holy water but without the salt.

Using sea water or ordinary salt water

To raise the energy levels in your home generally, you can add sea water (collect it as the tide is coming in) or salt water to your final laundry rinse, add it to the water you wash the floor with, sponge down the furniture and walls with it, add it to your bath water, and so on. Swimming in the sea is a wonderful way of purifying yourself.

Water spraying

Another way that I use water to revitalize a flagging atmosphere is by using an atomizer to spray a mixture of pure spring water with a few added drops of lavender essential oil up into the air. This helps to negatively ionize the air, as well as adding the fragrant scent of lavender, known for its uplifting qualities. It works as an instant "pick-me-up," and many therapists and workshop leaders like to use it between sessions to revive their atmospheres.

Using water sprayers generates negative ions that can counterbalance excessive positive ions being generated in homes and offices by televisions, computers, and other kinds of electrical equipment. In this circumstance, spray downward toward the floor to avoid getting water into the equipment.

Drink lots of water!

Remember to drink lots of water before and after you do Space Clearing, and anything else you do that involves working with energies. This keeps your own body flushed through, which produces a better result.

One reason why most westerners tend not to drink enough fluids is because we do not get excited about drinking the flat, lifeless water we get through our faucets or even spring water that has been stored in a bottle. We instinctively know that the vital essence of these types of water has dissipated. There is a world of difference between tap water and fresh, bubbling mountain spring water.

To reenergize your water and add more zest to your life, take a tip from the ancient Indian Hindu yogic practice of prana-ization. Pour the water quickly through the air from one glass to another several times before drinking to add new "life."

A nighttime glass of water

To improve your sleep, put a glass of water on a table near your head to absorb impurities around you while you sleep. For extra effect you can add a little bit of salt to the water. Don't drink the water! Throw it away in the morning. If you want to have drinking water near you while you sleep at night, have it in a sealed container such as a bottle or a cup that has a lid on it.

Purifying baths

The Christian religion has the practice of total immersion in water, known as baptism, as a means of spiritual purification. You can take a purifying bath in your own home.

You may choose to do this when you have no commitments the next day because you will get the best results if you don't have another bath or wash your hair for twenty-four hours after taking the bath. Some of the ingredients you may decide to use won't leave your hair looking like you just came out of a beauty salon!

First, clean the bathtub thoroughly. Don't use the bath to wash yourself as you usually would with soap afterward, or add any extra bath ingredients such as foam or oil. This bath is specifically for spiritual cleansing and purification. Brush your skin with a dry skin brush before climbing into the bathtub so that your skin is glowing (remember to brush toward the heart).

As the bathtub is filling, have a clear intention of what it is you want to release and let go of. Totally immerse yourself and visualize that the water is purifying you completely. Stay in the bathtub until you feel the process is complete, which may be a few minutes or a few hours. With a little practice and the right kind of plumbing fixtures, you can learn how to add more hot water using your feet without even having to sit up! When you get out of the bathtub, allow your body to drip dry. If the room is cold, just put on a bathrobe and wrap your hair in a towel.

Here are some ideas for different types of baths.

BAKING SODA/EPSOM SALTS BATHS

Bicarbonate of soda is used in baking as a rising agent, and you can add it to your bath water to raise your spirits and general state of health too! About a quarter of a cup is generally the right amount to add to your bath water. For extra oomph, double the quantity of baking soda, add a tablespoon of salt or a pint of sea water, and a cup of Epsom salts. This type of bath has a deeply cleansing and purifying effect. Have the water as hot as possible and cool off afterward with a cold shower.

HERBAL BATHS

Fresh herbs are obviously the most potent, but dried herbs for most purposes are fine. Just put a couple of teaspoons of the herb in a small teapot, add boiling water, allow to stand for ten minutes or so, strain the liquid into a jug, and pour it into the bathtub. It is nicest if you can keep all the bits of herbs out so that you don't have anything floating around in the bathtub. Try chamomile to relax and uplift you, or rosemary to combat fatigue. Sage is said to help you acquire wisdom, and ginger is excellent if you have a cold or the flu.

ESSENTIAL OIL BATHS

With this kind of bath you absorb the healing properties of the essential oils directly through your skin into your bloodstream and also inhale the fragrant aromas through your nose. Aromatherapy oils have a wide range of uses, and it is worth reading a book on the subject to select the most appropriate oils for you. Always check that the oils you select are suitable for adding to bath water.

FLOWER ESSENCE BATHS

Flower essences are homeopathically prepared remedies that treat the mental and emotional causes of disease or unhappiness. The first remedies were created in the 1930s by an English Harley Street doctor called Dr. Edward Bach, who identified thirty-eight flowers that could be used to treat fear, uncertainty, loneliness, despondency, despair, oversensitivity, jealousy, and a whole range of other states of mind and emotions. (Interestingly enough, the method he used to determine which plants were appropriate is exactly the same method I use when taking energy readings in buildings—this is described in the book *The Medical Discoveries of Edward Bach, Physician* by Nora Weeks.)

A treatment bottle consists of a few drops of one or more of the remedies added to spring water. This mixture is taken internally, a few drops at a time, several times a day. For extra effect, you can add drops to your bathwater, choosing the remedies you are already taking internally or choosing others. The Bach Flower Remedy prepared from Crab Apple flowers is a great cleanser, and Walnut is excellent for psychic purification. You may also like to try other similar types of remedies, such as Australian Bush Flower Essences.

FLOWER PETAL BATHS

If you want to give yourself a real treat, go out and buy huge amounts of beautiful fragrant flowers. Keep the petals and discard the rest. Float the petals in a container full of spring water so that they stay fresh. Have your partner, a friend, or a practitioner come to your home and give you a wonderful deep relaxing massage. After the massage, run a nice deep warm bath, throw in all the flower petals, and jump in yourself. Soak for as long as you want, inhaling the fragrant aroma of the flower petals and feeling them gently caress your skin as they float around you. Scoop up a handful of petals and rub them over your skin, absorbing their essence. This is one of the most spiritually uplifting baths you can take. This body treatment originated in Indonesia, where it was reserved only for royalty.

ENERGIZE YOUR BATH WATER

You can prana-ize your bath water just as you can prana-ize your drinking water simply by swishing your hands around in it! Most children intuitively do this anyway.

Alcohol

Alcohol is known in some cultures as "fire water"! It is a powerful purifier but needs to be treated with great care because it is highly flammable.

Strong rice wine is traditionally used in both China and Bali as an offering to the lower spirits of the earth. Rum can be substituted for rice wine for use in Western ceremonies. You can use it to add extra power to a consecration ceremony by pouring it on the ground in front of the house and in the four corners of the plot of land your house is built on.

PURIFICATION BY AIR

Air quality is very important in Space Clearing work, both in terms of its physical life-enhancing properties and also in terms of the energy content of the astral light (see Chapter 4). In the same way that we need to oxygenate our blood with the best quality of air that we can get, we also need to nourish our energy bodies with the highest levels of the astral light we can.

Different smells connect us to different levels of the astral light. The foul smell of rotting garbage is very low and obnoxious to us but heavenly to the creatures that inhabit that same level of the astral light. Higher levels of smells connect us to higher levels of the astral light and are inviting to the unseen worlds of healing presences, elementals, and so on.

Incense

Incense is used in most of the major religions of the world because it is a quick, easy way of raising the vibrational level of an atmosphere. Some incenses have very high frequencies, whereas others (especially synthetic varieties of incense) can actually lower the vibration or keep it at a mundane level. The thing to remember about incense is that it is actually only effective for as long as its aroma is in the air, so for Space Clearing it is best used in conjunction with other techniques rather than by itself. Light it when you first begin the Space Clearing procedures and keep it burning throughout. It is important to use an incense that you like the smell of, and there are two types in particular that are recommended for this work.

STICK INCENSE

The stick incense I use most often for Space Clearing used to be called Nitiraj Nagchampa and has just been renamed Nitiraj Original (see Resources section). Even people who never normally like incense invariably like this one. It is hand-rolled, has a wonderful, distinctive smell, is made of a unique blend of natural oils, gums, wood powders, herbs, and spices, and does the job beautifully. For safety reasons, remember to use an incense holder when you burn incense sticks inside the home and keep them well away from flammable materials.

GRANULAR INCENSE

Another incense I recommend is Basilica, which is used in Christian churches and is available from suppliers of church equipment. This is a tree resin that comes in the form of granules, and I use it when I need to do very deep cleansing work in a place. The best way to burn it is to light a self-igniting charcoal block, wait until it is glowing red hot, and then sprinkle the incense on top of it. The resin melts and starts to give off a beautiful wispy smoke, which you can then waft around the space.

It is important to use a receptacle that is suitable for this purpose. In my early Space Clearing days, I used to use an old frying pan, throw in three or four charcoal blocks and loads of incense, and walk around my home with smoke billowing all over the place. Next I progressed to using a censer—the swinging type of incense burner used in Christian churches—which was very effective. However, many people have negative associations with religious paraphernalia, so nowadays I use a small brass pan with a lid, which was originally designed for roasting chestnuts and does the job beautifully!

The charcoal block stays hot for a long time after the incense has finished smoking, so be sure to douse it under running water until it is extinguished or leave it to burn out in a place where it will not scorch the surface or cause a fire hazard.

Smudge sticks

Although I rarely use these, some people prefer to burn smudge sticks rather than incense. Smudging comes from the Native American tradition, and smudge sticks usually consist of a combination of dried herbs such as

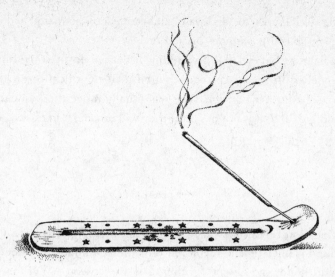

An incense holder

sage, mint, pine, cedar, sweetgrass, and others. They work in exactly the same way as incense.

Essential oils

I find that vaporized essential oils are too subtle for Space Clearing work, but they are wonderful to use after the space is clear to create and maintain fine new atmospheres. Fill the bowl of a ceramic vaporizer with water and add a few drops of your chosen essential oil or oils. A nightlight burning in the cavity below will slowly vaporize the oil and water mixture so that the aroma is released into the atmosphere for several hours. Always use pure, natural essential oils rather than synthetics.

PURIFICATION BY FIRE

Just sitting by an open fire will purify your emotions and cleanse your energy body. Fire is the only one of the four elements that purifies and yet stays pure itself. Earth, air, and water all become contaminated and need to be refreshed, but fire just goes on and on.

The Balinese believe that if a building is burned down, something must have happened in the place that required major purification. If they rebuild, to avert further disasters they will usually move the foundations of the building or, if that is not possible, they will rename it to change the frequency of the place.

Fire ceremonies

Fire purification ceremonies have formed an integral part of many of the great religions since time immemorial. The Indian Hindus conduct fire ceremonies to honor the Divine Mother. The fire is seen as her mouth, the source from which all things come, and making offerings to be burned in the fire is a way of giving back to her. Offerings may consist of rice, ghee (clarified butter), yogurt, honey, sugar, flowers, fruit, and sacred herbs, and the ceremony is immensely purifying, especially if done consciously using sacred mantras. Traditionally, a fire pit is dug in the ground, or a copper vessel called a *haven kund* can also be used.

Hearth fires

It is no coincidence that "hearth" and "heart" are such similar words. A hearth fire really puts heart into a home, and it says much about our culture that the television rather than the hearth fire has become the focal point of most of our modern Western homes.

If you have a hearth fire and you have the chimney regularly cleaned, you will find that the room it burns in generally needs less Space Clearing than other rooms, depending on the type of fuel you are burning. Smokeless fuel, while better for the environment, is not as effective in this respect as the stimulating, aromatic smells of a natural log fire, especially if you add purifying herbs such as sage. Food cooked on a wood fire also tastes better. In most urban areas of the world, however, wood fires are prohibited by clean air legislation. And any kind of hearth fire is actually an incredibly inefficient method of heating since about 90 percent of the heat is lost up the chimney!

Candles

Whenever you light a candle, always take the opportunity to dedicate it to something. You can say, "In lighting this candle, I now summon the angels of peace and harmony into this place," or "As I light this candle, may all who live in this place be blessed." You can find whatever words are appropriate to your situation.

Candles are vital to Space Clearing ceremonies because the act of lighting them activates the whole thing. As you place each offering in position and light the candle, this is an important moment to focus your intention in performing the ceremony.

For basic Space Clearing you put candlelit offerings in all the main rooms of the building. You will experience an even greater uplift in the vibration of the space if you position extra offerings in such a way that they form an illuminated energy matrix around the whole building. In other words, when you stand by one lighted candle, you can always see the next one, and when you move to that one you can see the next one in line, and so on. To achieve this, some candles will be positioned in rooms and others will be located in passageways to form connection points between the candles in rooms.

Always ensure that lighted candles can burn safely.

10.

Purification by Intention, Light, and Love

These intangible extras are the magic ingredients of Space Clearing, and the more you can infuse them into the ceremonies that you perform, the more profound your results will be.

PURIFICATION BY INTENTION

Knowledge applied with a clear desire and intention is one of the most powerful things on earth. You can read this book and go and clap out your home and ring a few bells in a very casual kind of way, and doing so will doubtless disperse some levels of stuck energy. But if you perform the ceremony with the strong intention that you are clearing the space for something specific that you want to come into your life, the results resonate far deeper and clear the way for transformational changes in your life.

PURIFICATION BY LIGHT

We all know intuitively that our quality of life is better if our home is filled with light. Stuck energy accumulates far more easily in a gloomy basement than it does in a sunny apartment.

To deep-cleanse a space, visualize that every part of it is filled with light, especially nooks and crannies, and anywhere there is dirt or grease, which is where low-energy forms love to hang out (ideally, physically clean these areas before Space Clearing).

For extra effect, burn camphor. The remarkable thing about camphor is that when it is burned, it leaves no residue whatsoever. It is used in *puja* in Indian Hindu temples to make an offering of light to the gods, and even to place small quantities of unlit camphor in small containers in the four corners of a room will have a profoundly purifying effect. Its aroma acts at a very deep level. Beware of using camphor if you are taking any homeopathic remedies because it will instantly neutralize them!

PURIFICATION BY LOVE

Love is the most powerful purifier of all. When we have love in our hearts we not only heal ourselves, but that frequency goes out from us and resonates with everything and everyone around us. We affect the electromagnetic fields of our homes, of the earth, and of all other beings. The heart creates an electromagnetic field that affects the state of our physical, emotional, mental, and spiritual well-being. Heart frequencies can be measured on ECG (electrocardiogram) machines, and scientists have now confirmed that far and away the most beneficial frequency to hold in one's heart is that of love and the most destructive is that of fear.

Do Space Clearing with all the love you can muster. Never be tempted, for example, to skimp on the quantity of candles, incense, and flowers you use, because you only cheat yourself. If you know in your heart that the space needs six candles and you can afford six candles, then *use* six candles. Conversely, if your resources only run to one candle and you know genuinely in your heart that you have done the best you can, that one candle will be all that you need.

In her book, *You Can Heal Your Life*, Louise L. Hay gives a wonderful affirmation that deeply affected me the first time I read it and continues to do so to this day:

I love myself; therefore, I provide for myself a comfortable home, one that fills all my needs and is a pleasure to be in. I fill the rooms with the vibration of love so that all who enter, myself included, will feel this love and be nourished by it.

Do your Space Clearing with love and then continue to pour love into your home on a daily basis. Another of Louise Hay's affirmations is:

The more love I use and give, the more I have to give, the supply is endless.

All the love you put into your home will return to you multiplied because really it is you loving you, you taking care of you. Also, when you love and take care of yourself, you have so much more to give to others. The circle of love goes on and on.

PART THREE

Deeper Levels of Creating Sacred Space

11

How to Leave
an Old Home and
Move to a New One

The first two parts of this book are about basic levels of Space Clearing, which I have explained in some detail. This next part is an introduction to some of the more advanced levels and other applications of this work, to give an indication of its range and scope, and to show how creating sacred space can be integrated into your life.

CHOOSING A NEW HOME

It used to be that people were born, lived, and died all in the same house or at least the same neighborhood. This is very rare in our society nowadays. Most people move at some time, and some people move frequently. They are being drawn to move to a certain type of home in a certain type of place because their Higher Self knows that this is the ideal space for them to learn something in or because they have something karmic to complete. You may say, "Oh, but I didn't choose to live here, I'm only here because I can't afford anywhere better/my partner chose it/the apartment came with the job" or whatever, but on a higher level there is more going on.

Often I am asked to carry out a Feng Shui survey of a property someone is interested in buying. I have lost count of the number of times I have had to report back to them that if they moved to this building they would simply be re-creating the same situation they already have so it would not be a progression for them.

In truth, we all do this in many aspects of our lives. We keep creating similar partners, or similar bosses, or similar situations, until hopefully we finally learn the lesson that our Higher Self is trying to teach us. The unconscious person may live a lifetime, of course, and still never grasp the pattern that is being presented. Some people create major traumas in their lives in order to get the point. Gill Edwards, author of *Living Magically*, has a wonderful phrase. She says, "If you listen to the whispers, you don't have to hear the screams." In other words, if you listen to the subtle suggestions of your Higher Self, you can give yourself a much easier time.

One of my clients lived in a house that had the far right-hand corner missing all the way up the building. If you consult the diagram of the Feng Shui bagua later on in the book, you will see that the whole Relationships area of her home was missing and, sure enough, that was the big issue in her life. She was anxious to move to a new house and begged me to come quickly and look at a property she had found. You've guessed it—the new home had exactly the same area missing. I walked in and walked out, and that was the end of the consultation. She was amazed she hadn't spotted it herself, but of course we are often blind to these things ourselves. We tend to go around and around the circle of life until we learn the lesson, and this includes the homes and workspaces that we choose for ourselves.

I wonder when someone will open a twenty-first century real-estate agency, where all properties are doused, surveyed by a Feng Shui consultant, Space Cleared, and consecrated so that they can be matched to the individual needs of clients. My sense is that it will happen very soon.

LEAVING AN OLD HOME

When you make a decision to move, a part of your energy goes on ahead of you into the future, searching for that new space. This can have repercussions energetically in your relationship with your present home. For example, because you have withdrawn your commitment to staying in the place, you may decide that there is therefore no point in finishing off painting that room you started or repairing that leaky faucet. You may save yourself a little time and money, but actually you will be doing yourself a greater disservice. You are connected to everything that you own, and the most numerous connections are to the place you call home. When you neglect your home environment, you neglect yourself. If the atmospheres in your home become depleted and dull, it becomes more difficult to manifest positive changes in your life.

If you have decided to move but can't seem to make it happen, look to see whether this may be the reason. When you put love and care into the place you live and are grateful for what you have, your cup runneth over and produceth more! You can still put energy into what you want for the future, but not at the expense of what you have now.

Something else I have noticed can happen when people decide to move is that they are burglarized. They make the decision to move, withdraw energetically from the space and, in so doing, can give out a signal that burglars pick up on. They read it as an invitation to pay a call!

Nighttime visualization

Here is a visualization you can do before you go to sleep at night to ensure this does not happen. It is also a wonderful process to do every night of your life to maintain clear, vibrant atmospheres in your home. It works best if you have already shielded your home during Space Clearing.

As you are lying in bed getting ready to go to sleep, close your eyes and visualize yourself stepping out of your body and standing beside the bed. Fill the whole room with clear, shimmering light and positive, vibrant energy. Go into each room in your home in turn and fill each room with this light and energy. You can easily glide through doors, walls, floors, and ceilings to accomplish this! When you have finished, return to your bed, slip back into your body, and go to sleep. With practice you will be able to do this in a matter of seconds.

FINDING A NEW HOME

Soon after I started spending half of each year in Bali and half of each year in England, I sold my London apartment and started trusting in the universe to provide me with suitable accommodation each time I returned from the tropics. A few weeks before leaving Bali each year, Rai and I sit down and write a list of our requirements, as specifically as we can. For example, we may need a one-bedroom apartment near Hampstead, with an extra room I can use as a study, a nice garden, easy parking, friendly neighbors, close to a subway station, with beautiful furniture and a cat we can borrow if we'd like to. It has to be at a price we can easily afford and available immediately for as long as we want it.

You can use exactly the same method to find a new home to rent or buy. It is important that as you do it you have a deep inner certainty that this new home exists and you will discover it soon. Of course you usually have to put some effort into finding it. You may have to scan advertisements, make a few phone calls, and so on. You can also enhance the Helpful Friends area of the bagua of your present home (see Part Five of this book).

MOVING TO A NEW HOME

Finding your new home is only the beginning of the process. Moving can be a traumatic experience, because we can form such strong emotional attachments to places we live in. One way to ease this transition is to take the happiest memories with you when you go.

Try to arrange timings with your movers and the new buyer or tenant so that you can have your old home to yourself for a while after everything has been taken out. It is good karma to leave your home as you would wish to find it (if you do this you will generally find that other people do the same for you), so take some time to do any necessary cleaning.

Next, go around and Space Clear your entire home. This is more good karma for you, because you are leaving the place not only physically clean but also psychically clear for the next people who will live there. Once you know how to do Space Clearing, it feels irresponsible not to clean up after yourself in this way.

Space Clearing breaks up the lower levels of vibrations but leaves the higher levels intact. All your happy memories in your home are therefore still intact, and these are the memories you may like to take with you to the next place.

Go into each room and say goodbye. You may like to pat the walls or the doors affectionately. Banisters are good to stroke because you will have touched them many, many times already while you have been living there. If you are not a particularly tactile person, you may like to say verbal goodbyes and thank yous, or you may prefer to simply take one last look. If you feel emotional, let those emotions surface. It's better to cry a few tears at the right time than to ache for years with feelings bottled up inside.

When you feel complete with this, stand in the middle of one of the rooms and stretch out your arms on either side of you at shoulder height. Concentrate on expanding your aura to the farthest parts of the room so that you fill the whole space. Connect with the highest energy of the place and your happiest memories there. Then, keeping your arms at shoulder height, sweep them toward yourself in two wide circular arcs, wrapping the energy around you like a beautiful warm cloak. Let your hands meet and cross, place them over your heart, and put those happy memories inside your heart.

Go into each room in the house in turn. If you can find a spot in the house where you feel you can stand and connect with the whole space simultaneously, you only need to do this once. Do what feels best to you.

You can keep this energy safely in your heart for a long, long time if necessary. You may want to get your new home looking great before you unfold these memories into the new space, and it is certainly a good idea to Space Clear the new place first. When you are ready, stand in a central place or go into each room in turn, and unfold the energy you have been keeping in your heart. Stand with your hands over your heart and gradually unfurl your arms as if you were opening out a big cloak. You will feel at home very quickly.

TAKING YOU WITH YOU

If you travel a lot, you will love this next tip. I learned it from Rai the first time he came to England with me. When he was leaving to go back to Bali, he went to our bed and did the most marvellous thing. He threw himself upon it spread-eagled in a passionate embrace, which was his way of giving thanks for all the wonderful nights of sleep and hours of pleasure we had shared in that space together. Then he sat up in the middle of the bed and, using his right hand, he stroked the bed and then put his hand to his heart and held it there. He did this three times with his attention focused on his heart chakra. It was very moving to watch.

"What are you doing?" I asked, intrigued.

"I'm taking me with me, of course," he said.

"And what will you do when you get back to Bali?" I asked.

He looked at me as if I had a screw missing. "This, of course!" he said, doing the action in reverse, taking the energy from his heart and putting it back into the bed. So simple and so effective.

As I said, this is a useful practice to know if you go traveling and also if you live in a furnished room and cannot take your bed with you if you move. It allows you to carry your own center with you wherever you go and may account for the fact that Balinese people can happily sleep anywhere.

CONSCIOUS REDECORATING

One very effective way of putting your energy into your new home is to totally redecorate. Conscious redecorating involves consciously dedicating your house as you do the work by putting specific frequencies into the walls as you go. If you do not want or are unable to do your own decorating but would like to make the best use of the decorating process, choose workers whose energy you like and energize the cans of paint before they start work. You can do this before they arrive for work in the morning if you don't want to appear weird. Simply take the can of paint between your hands, focus on what you want to energize it with, and allow the essence of that to flow out of your hands and into the can. You can also use visualization to put images into the can, and if you enjoy working with sound you can speak or tone them into the paint.

12.

Consecrating a Space

Ideally it is best to decorate and/or refurbish your new home first, then
hold a consecration ceremony, and then move in. In practice it may not
happen in this order. It is perfectly all right to move in, consecrate the
space, and then redecorate, but you will usually find that after all the work
is finished, it is beneficial to reconsecrate or at least do the basic Space
Clearing procedures again. This will allow your atmospheres to settle and
your energies to anchor in the space. The basic Space Clearing I outlined
in the earlier part of this book is a shortened version of a complete consecration ceremony.

For many of you it will be the case that you have already lived in your
home for many years before you read this book and would now like to consecrate it. You certainly can do this, and I encourage you to do so. First you
will need to know how to create an altar in your home.

CREATING AN "ALTAR" IN YOUR HOME

Creating an altar is an effective way of anchoring energies in your home in
order to maintain high-level atmospheres. During a consecration ceremony you will be calling higher presences into your space, and in much

the same way that you prepare a room for a guest who is coming to stay, you need to prepare a space that feels welcoming.

Choose a place that has a nice feel to it and position your altar where you can safely burn candles and incense. If you have a religious affiliation, you can choose to put things on your altar that relate to your beliefs. The important thing is to have items that are special and meaningful to you and that represent the energies you wish to gather to yourself. You may have a special cloth you would like to use, a crystal you feel a particular affinity for, a leaf you picked up off the earth at a significant time in your life, or a particular ornament that inspires you. You may include significant symbols, mantras, photographs, and so on. For the consecration ceremony you will need to have room on the altar to place offerings and incense.

CONSECRATION CEREMONY FOR A NEW HOME

Many elements can be included in this ceremony. As with basic Space Clearing, I will give you a step-by-step series of procedures to follow, which you can vary and add to as you deem appropriate. Here is an example of a ceremony to consecrate a Western house.

1. Ideally, all members of your household will be present to assist you as you consecrate the space.
2. Follow the same preparations as for basic Space Clearing, paying particular attention to Step 5 of the checklist (each person needs to be very clear on what they want to have happen in this new space and write it down).
3. Everyone needs to be freshly bathed and be wearing fresh, clean clothing.
4. Put some holy water on your head, hands, and feet and take some incense into your auric field.
5. Dig a small hole in the ground in front of the house (for the earth spirits) and create a special altar inside the house (for the guardian spirit of the house, other helpers, and higher

presences). Have candles and incense burning at these two
places throughout the ceremony.

6. Put salt in the hole, at each corner of the plot of land on
which the house is built, scatter it on every threshold (especially the main entrance), along all the window ledges, in
every corner of every room, and wherever else you feel it is
needed.

7. Place flowers, fruit, or rice or other kinds of food in the ceremonial hole as an offering to the spirits of the earth, together with a gift from each of you (it can be money, a
personal possession, or something else you feel is appropriate). Sprinkle holy water on the offerings.

8. Place similar offerings and something that symbolizes spirit
to each of you on the altar inside the house and sprinkle
them with holy water too.

9. Put offerings of flowers, candles, incense, and holy water in
every room and at intersections within the building. Create
an illuminated energy matrix as described in the section
about candles in Chapter 9.

10. Perform the Basic Space Clearing procedures, up to Step 6.

11. Sit or stand by your altar. Balance your chakras and each
member of your household's chakras with a good quality
bell or center yourselves by whatever method you prefer.

12. Place your lists of what qualities or happenings you want to
manifest in your new home on the altar. Each of you takes a
harmony ball and cups it between your hands. Read aloud in
turn or read silently to yourselves what you choose to consecrate the space to (decide between yourselves which
method you prefer). Close your eyes and image this into
your harmony balls. Sense it, feel it, taste it, smell it, know
it. Then take the harmony balls and shake them into the
whole building, room by room. Your intention is powerful.
As you think, so you create.

13. Offer thanks to unseen helpers and light a seven-day candle
on your altar to attract and anchor energies while you are all
settling into the new space.

14. Sprinkle some holy water on the heads of the members of your household. If the holy water is from a source that is suitable for drinking, drink some yourself, give some to the others and also include any pets. Put the holy water in their drinking water or put some behind their ears or on their paws.

15. Scatter flower petals across every threshold. Use a flower head to sprinkle holy water on top of the flowers (especially across the main entrance), around the entire inside perimeter of the house and in the center of each room.

16. Sprinkle some holy water in the ceremonial hole and fill it in with earth. Finally, sprinkle holy water around the inside perimeter of the plot of land.

17. Leave all the candles and incense to safely burn out and leave all the flowers and the salt overnight or longer if you wish.

Parts of this ceremony have been adapted from a typical Balinese consecration ceremony. One of the major differences is that in Bali very elaborate offerings for the gods and food for the many invited guests would be prepared, which would take at least a whole day and night, and then the ceremony itself would take another full day to perform. At all the consecration ceremonies I have attended, everyone cheerfully stays awake throughout the night and the whole of the next day to contribute their skills to the happy occasion. I don't think it is necessary to do this in the West, but it is good for every member of the household to contribute to the ceremony in some way.

13.

Bringing More
Sacredness into
Your Life

Everything has a meaning. Let me put it another way: there is nothing that does not have a meaning. The fact that I have chosen to write this sitting at this particular table in this particular restaurant at this particular time all has a meaning. All the events of my life have led to this point in time, which contains all possibilities for the future. My attention determines the depth and quality of my experience.

I am always intensely interested in everything that is happening around me because it provides me with all the information I need about what is happening within me. For example, if the meal I have ordered turns out to be not what I had hoped for, I know that something is out of balance in me. Were it not so, I would have chosen a different meal or a different restaurant, or a different person would have cooked the meal, and so on. Well, just so that you know, in the time it has taken me to write this my meal has arrived, and it is delicious. My life is on track.

THE SACRED DANCE OF LIFE

I believe that each of us has a Higher Self that goes ahead of us and sets up situations that we need in order to learn the things we need to learn. When you live in close communication with your Higher Self, life becomes a sacred dance and a joy. The universe (*uni-verse*, literally "one song") shows us in every way it can provide everything we need to know for our journey through life.

The natural progression of purifying the energy in your home is to make all your life sacred so that everything has a meaning and a purpose. You start with your home and then you'll want to go further.

Space Clearing has to do with raising levels of consciousness. By cleansing your atmospheres, you create a sacredness around you rather than just living at a mundane level. What we've lost in the West is the specialness of things. We just move into a new house with no respect for the land or the building, or each other. We've lost the sacredness of life. So I call what I do "creating sacred space" because it is bringing back the magic into our relationship with our homes.

CEREMONIES

One of the things people find so charming about Bali is the ceremonial way of life. Ceremonies appeal to something deep inside of us that longs for expression. They reach deep inside us and touch our spirituality. When ceremonies become a part of everyday life, we can experience feelings of deep contentment and belonging. Children naturally create ceremonies. Some people go to a place of religious worship for ceremonies, and others prefer to create their own. You can take something as simple as brushing your teeth and create a ceremony around it if you decide that the time you brush your teeth is going to be the time when you focus your attention on something you want to create or change in your life. This is how you can start to make your life sacred.

Rituals are different from ceremonies. I use the word *ceremony* for those acts that are so irresistible to the unseen worlds that they love to come and join you. Rituals are acts that are performed to force entities to come, and this can be dangerous if you bite off more than you can chew.

The more often a ceremony or ritual is repeated, the more powerful it becomes.

MAKING THINGS SACRED

Stuart Wilde, a prolific and charismatic author and metaphysical teacher, has a lovely way of putting it. In his book, *The Secrets of Life*, he has a passage entitled, "On making life sacred":

> How does something become sacred? It becomes sacred by people saying, "This is sacred." There is no other way. So St. Matilda's toenail in a box is just that, until someone says, "This relic is holy and special." So how do you make your life sacred? You say, "This is sacred," and you treat it that way.

You can make things sacred and bond with things, and love them and enjoy them, and your life will be all the richer for it. I am a great one for making things special, but the trick to it is doing it without attachment. You can have a special crystal but realize you can never own it. It belongs to the planet. You can use it while you are in a physical body, you can even bequeath it to someone after you die, but ultimately it will return to the planet from whence it came just as you will return to spirit from whence you came.

You can create consecration ceremonies for anything that is special to you by tuning in to it and intuiting what would be appropriate.

Creating sacred space for children

The Balinese usually put a small offering box called a *plankiran* over the sleeping place of a small child, and in it they will place offerings and talismans to ensure the safety of the child. A piece of the child's umbilical cord will be put in a small white pouch and kept there while the child is growing up, and there will be an inscription over the bed asking the gods to look after the child. The umbilical cord idea may never catch on in Western circles, but the inscription is a wonderful idea. A suitable wording might be: "This Child Is Protected and Blessed All the Days of His/Her Life." Imagine the deep sense of security a child would grow up with, knowing this was so.

Bonding with your home

Make friends with your home! Get tactile with it! Stroke the walls sometimes as you pass. Say "hello" when you arrive home. Learn to know what it needs to make it feel good.

If Prince Charles can talk to plants (and he's certainly not alone in that), then talking to your home isn't so different. Many people have been talking to their cars for years! Ask any good mechanic and they will tell you that machines run better when people speak to them kindly and encourage them. Ask any company that supplies equipment and they will tell you that there are always people whose machines seem to break down, no matter how carefully the equipment is tested before shipping.

Naming things

When you name something, you form a much closer relationship with it. It then works better and supports you more. Name your home, name your car, name your computer, name all the major objects that you interact with on a daily basis. You can also name your plants, your favorite crystals, and outfits that you have.

Choose names that match the essence of the object. As an example, "The Red Dragon" was a beautiful big, red Jaguar sedan I once owned; "Peanut" was a tiny peanut-shaped Volkswagen, which cost me peanuts to buy and run; and "Three Piece" was a Peugeot sedan with tweed seats, which looked (and felt) like a three-piece suit on wheels. I almost never have the experience of cars breaking down on me because, in accepting them into my life, they become part of my energy matrix. If I am healthy, they are healthy. I nourish and maintain them in the same way that I nourish and maintain myself.

If you move into a new home that has already been given a name by your predecessors, check that it is appropriate for what you want to happen in the space. The name of the street, the district, the town, and so on can also have an enhancing or detrimental effect.

The process of naming is the art of being able to match frequencies of sounds with frequencies of things. There is always a combination of consonants and vowels that will express the unique energy of your home, and all you have to do is tune in and find it. When you get the right name, it feels fantastic and allows you access to even deeper levels than before.

PART FOUR

Electromagnetic Awareness

14.

Geopathic Stress

In creating sacred space, it is important to take into account not just the building but also the energy emanating from the land it is built on, which can also have a tremendous effect on us.

LOCATION

Ask any real-estate agent what are the three most important selling features of any property and they will almost certainly tell you: "Location, location, location." Or in Chinese terminology, "Feng Shui, Feng Shui, Feng Shui." With increasing awareness of geopathic stress, the importance of location now takes on a new meaning.

Geopathic stress is the name given to the harmful effects of unstable or disrupted natural electromagnetic fields emanating from the earth. Extensive research in Europe over the last seventy years has led many experts there to conclude that being exposed to these rays for extended periods of time can weaken one's immune system and increase the risk of cancer and other chronic diseases.

In the process of compiling her authoritative book, *Earth Radiation*, Käthe Bachler dowsed over eleven thousand beds in over three thousand homes in fourteen countries and presents very convincing evidence to this effect. Similarly, Dr. Hager of the Scientific Association of Medical Doctors conducted a huge survey of the houses of 5,348 people who had died of cancer in the town of Stettin in Poland and established that strong earth rays crossed their homes in all cases. Myalgic encephalomyelitis, multiple sclerosis, arthritis, chronic depression, suicide, crib deaths, high blood pressure, and many other serious ailments have also been linked to geopathic stress.

Such a huge body of evidence has been built up in Germany, Austria, and France that many medical doctors now routinely do dowsing themselves or enlist the help of qualified dowsers to test that their patients' beds are safely positioned, and some Austrian authorities insist that plots of land are dowsed for harmful earth rays before they will give planning permission for certain kinds of buildings to be erected.

Harmful earth rays

There are several different types of earth rays. Some are global grids with names such as the Hartmann net (which runs in the same directions as our lines of latitude and longitude) and the Curry grid (intersecting diagonal lines running northeast/southwest and southeast/northwest), and harmful effects can occur at intersection points on these grids. Distortions of earth energies due to the movement of underground water streams can also cause problems, especially at points where two underground streams cross at different levels.

It is important to understand that these rays are not "bad." They are simply harmful to humans. Other life-forms thrive on them, as I will explain later.

Beneficial earth rays

Schumann waves are earth rays that promote good health, and the National Aeronautics and Space Administration (NASA) has had to create machines to simulate these waves in space capsules because humans can-

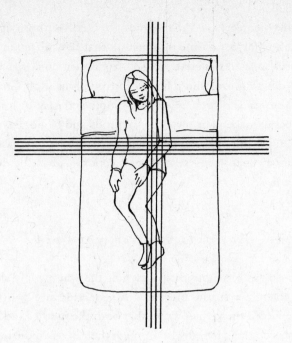

Geopathic stress lines crossing a bed

not survive without them. Unfortunately, Schumann waves are inhibited by modern building materials such as concrete, which presents a problem in urban areas and especially in high-rise buildings. Healthy people can normally handle this, but sick people or those under a lot of stress may benefit from using a Schumann wave simulator themselves.

HOW TO KNOW IF YOUR HOME HAS GEOPATHIC STRESS

Dowsing

If you or someone who lives with you becomes chronically ill and does not respond to treatment, it is very possible that geopathic stress is present. The easiest way to test for this is to employ the services of a professional dowser. Since some dowsers are more accurate than others, I usually recommend that people have their homes checked by three dowsers independently and only act on the information that they all agree on.

You can also learn to dowse yourself. Sig Lonegren's *Dowsing Rod Kit* includes two dowsing rods and a book of instructions. Rolf Gordon's book, *Are You Sleeping in a Safe Place?*, gives very simple and easy-to-follow instructions on how to make your own dowsing rods and begin dowsing in your own home. Dowsing rods and pendulums can also be purchased commercially and are inexpensive (see Resources section). Advanced dowsers need no equipment.

How you sleep in your bed

Apart from dowsing, simple things such as the way people sleep in their beds may give clues to the presence of geopathic stress. In one client's house I discovered through dowsing that both the mother and teenage son had earth rays crossing lengthwise through their beds. In the mother's case, the ray neatly dissected her king-size bed in two, and she confirmed that although she had slept alone ever since she had had the bed in that position, she never ever wanted to sleep in the middle of the bed. In the case of the son, he too admitted that he only ever slept on one side of his bed, which turned out to be the side that was free from geopathic stress.

People who are sensitive intuitively move away from geopathically stressed areas in their sleep. Time and time again I have had this confirmed by parents who find their baby or young child scrunched up at one end or one side of the bed every morning. They are trying to escape from harmful earth rays crossing through a section of the bed. Parents need to take note of this and immediately move the bed. Other clues are if the child frequently has nightmares, wakes up crying in the night, or wets the bed. There may be other causes involved, but geopathic stress should be investigated.

Pets

If you have a cat or a dog as a pet, they can often give clues as to where harmful rays are situated. Cats adore the energy and thrive on it, whereas dogs have a total aversion to it. If your cat loves sleeping in a certain spot, that is somewhere for you to avoid spending long periods of time. This does not necessarily mean, however, that if your cat loves sleeping on your bed that there must be geopathic stress in that area, because domesticated cats sometimes choose warmth, comfort, and closeness to their owner above the delights of lying on earth rays. However, if you move your bed and the cat still goes to the same position to sleep, you were almost certainly sleeping in a "bad" location. This, incidentally, explains why pets sometimes will not sleep in their beds. If your cat or dog won't sleep in the spot where you have placed their bedding, try moving it until you find a place where they will settle.

Ray seekers and ray avoiders

Bacteria, viruses, and parasites thrive on earth rays. They naturally congregate there and rapidly multiply. Ants, termites, bees, and wasps always prefer to site their nests at points where harmful earth rays cross.

Chickens, ducks, and most birds, on the other hand, do not like to be near earth rays and will usually become ill or even die. This gives new insight into the old saying that it is lucky to have a stork nest in your roof.

One client I visited had bought a bird and hung its cage in a corner of her sitting room. It soon died, cause unknown and so she replaced it. That one died too, and the next one. At this point she gave up on the idea of having a bird in the house. She told me this after I had dowsed the area and found harmful earth energies radiating up into that particular corner of the room. If she had only placed the cage a short distance away, the birds need not have died.

If you are fortunate enough to be able to build your own home, one way to check that key positions will be clear of geopathic stress is to use an old Bavarian technique. Place an anthill there. If the ants stay put, do not build; if they move away, you're OK.

Never build a home at a place where lightning has struck. This is because lightning always strikes where two subterranean streams cross at a substantial difference in depth. An old oak tree is not a good tree to shelter under in a thunderstorm because oak trees thrive at the crossing points of underground streams and are frequently struck by lightning.

Some trees do not thrive in geopathically stressed areas and will either contort unnaturally in an attempt to grow away or will develop cancerous growths and die. Fruit trees may blossom but never produce fruit. Cut flowers, when placed in areas that are geopathically stressed, will last only half as long as they normally would. Mechanical equipment placed over harmful earth rays frequently breaks down, and light bulbs repeatedly burn out.

WAYS TO NEUTRALIZE
GEOPATHIC STRESS

Avoid it in the first place

Rolf Gordon makes a very valid point: "When you buy a car you are normally allowed to test drive it. . . . Why do you not insist on sleeping a few nights in a house you propose to buy before you sign the contract?"

These days it is no longer sufficient to have a house you are thinking of buying surveyed just for soundness of structure, moisture, and the like. If you value your health and well-being, and you intend to live in that place for any length of time, check it over for geopathic stress. Pay particular attention to the areas where you are planning to put beds, desks, favorite armchairs, and anywhere else you will spend more than four hours a day. Having the place professionally dowsed is inexpensive compared to all the other expenses in buying a house and could be the most vital outlay of them all. What, after all, is the point of living in your ideal home if it is going to wreck your physical and emotional health? In Germany, where dowsing is taken very seriously, some builders now offer certificates to guarantee that vital areas in new houses have been dowsed and are free of geopathic stress.

It is interesting to note that in all the homes I have ever visited of people suffering with myalgic encephalomyelitis, they have geopathic stress lines crossing their bed, and for one reason or another it has been impossible to move their bed to any position other than the one they have it in.

Gadgets

A quick trip around any alternative health exhibition will reveal a number of different products claiming to neutralize geopathic stress. Most of these are well intentioned, but most are either ineffective or helpful only for a short period of time. Any devices installed always need to be checked periodically by dowsing to ensure they are still effective. One device developed by the Dulwich Health Society in the U.K., which many people claim has been effective in neutralizing geopathic stress in their homes, is called the RadiTech (see Resources). It has to be plugged into an electric socket and yet uses no electricity at all except to illuminate the pilot light. One device is usually sufficient to treat the whole house.

Insulation

Plastic and cork are good insulators and can help to gain emergency, short term relief from harmful earth rays. Spread plastic sheeting or untreated cork tiles between your box spring and your mattress. Depending on your sensitivity and the strength of the geopathic stress, the plastic sheeting will last a week or two before it needs replacing and the cork tiles a little longer. Note that if your bed frame is made of metal or your mattress has metal springs, and any part of it is in a geopathically stressed area, the metal will conduct the harmful radiation throughout the bed. For this and many other reasons, wooden beds and natural cotton mattresses are a far better choice.

Earth acupuncture

Some practitioners hammer lengths of copper piping, iron rods, or wooden wands into the ground at points where the rays enter a building. It works as if by magic. Within hours the geopathic stress has vanished.

Now, I'm willing to concede that in the case of toxic underground streams a great adept could bring neutralizing forces to bear that would be effective at least for a while. I'm also willing to concede that in the case of earth lines it is possible to divert them by this method. But both scenarios have dubious integrity. They smack of humans playing God with these great forces of Nature and take no account of where the energies are being diverted to (probably to your neighbor's house!). Just imagine the cumulative effect of hundreds of earth acupuncturists around the world making a small adjustment here and a small adjustment there. Imagine this continues for a hundred years and what do you have? Total chaos in Nature!

I confess I used to recommend this method sometimes. However I never practiced it myself. The results were great but something about it never felt quite right. Now I'm totally opposed to it and speak out about it whenever I can.

Feng Shui

Some Feng Shui practitioners and dowsers believe that it is building our buildings without regard for the geomancy (energy flows) of the land that has brought about such an increase in geopathic stress in Western countries in recent decades, causing natural earth rays to become harmful to human life. Another possibility is that the human immune system has been so weakened by modern living that these earth rays now damage our health. I tend to feel it is a combination of both.

In some cases, Space Clearing and correcting the flow of energies using Feng Shui helps to alleviate geopathic stress to some degree, depending on the consciousness and skill of the practitioner. However, this is not a cure. The only long-term remedy I ever recommend is to remove oneself from the vicinity of the stress (move your bed, move your chair, or in an extreme case, move house). One of the long-term aims of my work is to educate architects to design buildings that actually support people's health rather than endanger it.

Other methods of "healing" geopathic stress

As the incidence of geopathic stress in our environment increases many new teachers are emerging with techniques that claim to be a cure-all. I greet them all with a healthy dose of skepticism and encourage you to do the same.

PRECAUTIONS FOR DOWSERS

All rays have a much stronger effect at the points where they cross, at the time of the full moon, when there is sunspot activity going on, in the early hours of the morning, during rainy or stormy weather, and when there is substantial environmental pollution. Although it is easier to detect the rays at these times, it is not advisable to do so. Dowsing, at the best of times, has its inherent dangers, simply because to do it you have to put yourself on the same frequency as the harmful rays. Never dowse if you are ill or tired, and always take a bath or shower (or, at the very least, wash your hands under running water) after dowsing.

A safer way is to dowse for places that are beneficial rather than searching for harmful rays. I have found the results of this type of dowsing are just as accurate and have the effect of revitalizing rather than depleting one's energy.

15.

Electromagnetic

Stress

We are affected not only by geopathic stress resulting from distortions of natural electromagnetic emanations from the earth but also by the artificial electromagnetic fields (EMFs) generated by electrical equipment made by humans.

HUMANS AS
ELECTROMAGNETIC BEINGS

Humans are incredibly sensitive electromagnetic beings. Many years ago, near the beginning of the twentieth century and before our planet was drenched in the radio waves, microwaves, radar, television transmissions, computer systems, mobile phones, satellite, and cable transmissions that we now take for granted, an American physician named Albert Abrams created a machine called an oscilloclast, which measured muscular reactions in his patients' stomachs. He recorded that the muscles reacted to electrical signals as weak as turning on a machine in the same building. In other words, the human body is sensitive enough to react to electromagnetic fields at a distance. Nowadays we are bombarded by so many electromagnetic frequencies that we would have to build a specially insulated room to measure these reactions. This means that we no longer have any idea what "normal" feels like.

The World Health Organization confirms that "the human body emits electromagnetic fields at frequencies of up to 300 GHz." (*EHC 137: Electromagnetic fields*, WHO, Geneva, 1993). This encompasses the wavebands of all power lines, domestic and office equipment, mobile phones, radio transmissions, microwaves, radar, and even satellite transmissions. Some people are able to hear radar pulses, and there have been reported cases of radio broadcasts being clearly audible through the metal fillings in the mouths of people who live near broadcasting towers. Part of the pressure of modern day living is actually just handling the traffic of all these electromagnetic signals passing through us, which is estimated to be up to 200 million times more than our ancestors were exposed to.

HUMAN-MADE ELECTROMAGNETIC FIELDS

We all learn in school that an alternating electric current flowing through a wire creates a magnetic field around it. Electromagnetic stress is caused by exposing our bodies to either artificial or distorted natural EMFs, which penetrate and alter our cellular processes. The results of all my work lead me to conclude that this can affect the quality of people's vital life forces, and severe or long-term exposure can weaken their immune systems, leading to a breakdown in health.

Human-made EMFs can be detected with your hands in the same way that you can sense energies in buildings (try it and see). I have noticed consistently that when there is a larger than normal EMF around all the pieces of electrical apparatus in a home, some or all of the people living there invariably have impaired immune systems. The extent of the enlarged field allows me to determine how severely their immune system is affected, and by sensing the energy in the individual bedrooms it is usually possible to track down who has the problem.

The reason why I think the fields are enlarged is because a person with a normal healthy immune system can process and handle the electromagnetic stress of the apparatus that surrounds him or her, which keeps the EMF to a manageable size, but a person with an impaired immune system is not able to handle it, so the field grows. The electrical apparatus then has a greater effect on the person, which further weakens the immune system, and so on and on.

Western teenagers are often unknowingly bombarded with electromagnetic stress by surrounding themselves with lots of equipment, which can all be operated from their bed. In many homes, it is very common to find televisions, videos, computers, sound systems, clock radios, and other electrical gadgetry, which remains plugged in twenty-four hours a day in their bedrooms. Probably they are also using computers at school and subjecting themselves to other electromagnetic stresses too. I believe some of them become addicted to it. Caring parents become concerned about them because they never seem to have any energy or enthusiasm for anything. They become teenage couch potatoes.

No amount of parental nagging seems to get through to these teenagers, but one thing that does seem to make them sit up and take notice is a machine I have been using for the last couple of years that measures electric and magnetic fields. I show them what is considered to be a safe level and watch their jaws drop open as the needle goes off the dial when I walk around their bedroom with it.

Space Clearing helps to reduce the oversized EMFs temporarily, but they will build up again if something is not done to repair the immune systems of the affected people, and they continue to bombard themselves with the emissions of electrical apparatus.

HEALTH HAZARDS

Everyone knows that electricity is dangerous, and a severe electric shock can kill. It has taken a long time for governments to accept the evidence, but some are now gradually admitting that chronic exposure to electrical cables and equipment can be hazardous to health. This takes many forms, from unexplainable depression to debilitating physical side effects. There is growing evidence (eleven major studies to date), for example, linking prolonged exposure to Extremely Low Frequencies (ELF), such as those emitted by high-tension power lines, with life-threatening illnesses such as childhood leukemia. The most significant of these was the Swedish study by Feychting and Ahlbom, which concluded that children living close to power lines have two to five times the increased risk of leukemia.

It is important to understand that EMFs decrease with distance from the source, so the greatest dangers are posed by equipment we have to be close to in order to use or EMFs we are exposed to for long periods of time. As with geopathic stress, we need to be particularly alert to electromagnetic stress in areas where we spend several hours a day, and especially our sleeping places, where we may spend up to three thousand hours every year!

Jean Philips of Powerwatch, a United Kingdom pressure group concerned with the effects of electromagnetic radiation, explains that sleep "is the time when your body is going through a stage of cellular repair, when any abnormal cell activity is killed off by the immune system. We strongly believe radiation from certain appliances can disrupt this activity while you sleep, and it is a proven fact that abnormal cell growth can be carcinogenic" (*Daily Mail*, October 10, 1995).

EMFs in the workplace are another cause of concern. The World Bank certainly takes it seriously. Its headquarters in Washington, D.C., which covers an entire city block, was designed according to a "prudent avoidance" program. The main electrical switching equipment is situated in the fifth sub-basement, as far away from workers as possible, and the bank has found ways to limit exposures to all wiring and equipment generating EMFs. Another bank, Marine Midland, sued its landlord concerning floor-level power cables generating magnetic fields of up to 300 milligauss in its offices on Park Avenue in New York City. It cost the landlord one million dollars to shield the cables and bring the EMFs down to an acceptable level.

Understanding the jargon

The electricity supply most commonly found in Western homes is an alternating current pulsating at fifty or sixty cycles per second, which falls in the category of an ELF electromagnetic field. These fields are relatively weak in comparison to industrial supplies and so were considered safe, but current studies are providing cause for concern.

Roger Coghill, author of *Electropollution* and an authority on the subject, is committed to heightening public awareness of these dangers. The background magnetic field in Western homes doesn't usually exceed 1 or 2 milligauss, and the electric field is generally in the range of 2 to 5 volts per meter (V/m). However, the presence of nearby power cables can drastically increase these levels, and the EMFs of some types of ordinary household equipment are many times higher. Roger Coghill's extensive research has led him to conclude that "in magnetic fields above 2 milligauss and electric fields above 20 V/m, there is four to six times the elevated risk of cancer in small children and of nonspecific ill-health symptoms among adults." Researchers from government agencies in Scandinavia and the United States have arrived at similar conclusions.

An article in the *New Scientist* (October 7, 1995) listed the levels of exposure of some household appliances at a range of twelve inches. Vacuum cleaners are commonly in the range of 20-200 milligauss, washing machines 1.5-30 milligauss, electric ovens 1.5-5 milligauss, and hairdryers 0.1-70 milligauss. The strongest magnetic fields are produced by transformers (many electrical appliances have these).

Roger Coghill believes, however, that it is the electric field rather than the magnetic that does the most harm, but little government research or industry funding has been available to research this aspect yet. He has found that health starts to suffer when the electric field exceeds 10 V/m, and degenerative diseases are likely with long-term exposure to 20 V/m and above. Sleeping next to an electric heater, as an example, puts you in a field of up to 50 V/m. A small, inexpensive gadget called a FieldMouse allows you to test for safe levels of both fields in your own home, and more sophisticated instruments are also available for professionals such as surveyors and architects (see Resources section).

POWER CABLES

An advisory body to the United States government (the National Council for Radiation Protection) now recommends that schools are located well away from power cables because of the increased risk of leukemia. Make sure that no one in your home is sleeping or spending long periods of time near high-voltage power lines or pylons, some of which radiate EMFs up to a quarter of a mile on either side. The highest fields are found midway between pylons rather than around the pylon itself, and rooms at the top of a house are more affected than lower rooms. If choices are limited due to space, locate children's bedrooms farthest away from power cables, because they are more susceptible than adults. Walls, trees, and tall hedges between your home and the cables do help to counter some of the effects of electric fields by conducting them to earth but do not screen out magnetic fields, which simply pass through solid structures. Sleeping near electrical substations and end-of-line transformers also means increased exposure.

HOME APPLIANCES

Many kinds of electrical apparatus give rise to EMFs even when they are switched off because the electrons still flow up and down the circuit wiring to which they are attached. Get into the habit of unplugging appliances from the wall when you are not using them, or better still, install a device to cut off current at the source when the circuits are not in use. It is particularly good to install one of these for bedroom circuits in order to reduce your exposure to EMFs while you sleep.

Since there is almost always something electrical running in your home (the refrigerator, if nothing else), there is almost always an electrical current passing through your circuit box. Check that it is not located near where you spend extended periods of time, for example, near your bed, desk, or favorite armchair. Even if it is on the other side of a wall, you will be affected by the electromagnetic field.

Any equipment that is used to heat or cool generates strong EMFs around it. Don't sleep near an air conditioning unit, a refrigerator, or an electric water heater, or on the other side of a wall from one. Electric blankets are very convenient, but never keep them turned on all night. It's much better to use a good old-fashioned hot-water bottle or snuggle up to a partner for warmth. Metals concentrate the effects of magnetic fields and conduct electric currents, so have your bed at least four feet away from any metal water-filled radiators and even farther away from electric heaters if they are turned on at night.

Most people who sleep with a clock radio next to their bed find it difficult to wake up in the morning, and the problem usually improves when the equipment is moved. Clock radios emit surprisingly large EMFs for their size. Both the cord and the clock radio need to be at least eight feet away from your body, and particularly from your head, which is most susceptible to electromagnetic stress because it contains the body's most specialized EMF receptors, the retinas of the eyes and the pineal gland. It is much better for your health to use a battery-operated clock radio or wind-up alarm clock.

TELEVISIONS

The BBC television program *Tomorrow's World* once conducted a stunning experiment by taping a large lump of gold to the screen of a TV and leaving it switched on for two years. When it was removed on live national television, it was analyzed and found to have been converted to lead! The electrons emerging from the television screen seemed to have induced radioactive decay.

I heard recently that a new scheme has started whereby patients in English hospital beds may now rent personal televisions for the duration of their stay. The side effects of exposing patients to electromagnetic radiation clearly have not been considered. Color televisions emit large EMFs and can maintain their charge for up to several days, even after being unplugged from the wall.

If you must watch television, my advice is to do so for only a couple of hours a day, and certainly do not leave it turned on all the time "for company." Never sit right up close to a television. For an average-sized screen, six to ten feet away is the closest any part of your body should be (depending on the size of the screen, because larger screens emit larger EMFs), so position your armchairs accordingly. Children are particularly fond of sitting right up close to televisions, and one way to ensure that this doesn't happen is to mount it on a platform about six feet off the ground. If you are in the habit of watching TV stretched out in bed, your head may be far enough away from the screen but the rest of your body may not be!

Also learn to watch actively rather than passively. Falling asleep in front of the television is, in my view, a dangerous habit, because you cannot select what is going into your unconscious mind.

COMPUTERS

When you sit in front of a computer screen, you are being bombarded by many different emissions. These include visible light, ultraviolet light, VLF (Very Low Frequency) electromagnetic radiation, and ELF (Extremely Low Frequency) electromagnetic radiation. In some cases you are also being exposed to soft x-rays. Screens are supposed to filter these harmful rays, but all screens become less efficient at this as they get older, and there is also the problem of soft x-rays leaking from the sides and rear of the unit. Computer screens also emit positive ions that can cause "dry eye" and muscular aches of the arms and hands.

You can sit at a distance when watching TV but you must, of necessity, sit right next to a computer if you want to work with it. In Sweden it is now illegal for computer operators to use cathode ray tube screens with ELF fields exceeding 2.5 milligauss and 25 V/m, measured twenty inches from the computer screen in three planes. The Australian government recommends five hours per day as a safe maximum for computer work. In some parts of the United States pregnant women are not allowed to use computers in the workplace because of the high risk of miscarriage and birth defects, and some employers such as the National Union of Journalists and the BBC World Service recognize the dangers and will provide alternative work during pregnancy for any woman requesting it. Other possible hazards are menstrual disorders, loss of libido, infertility, breast cancer, eye problems, skin irritation, RSI (repetitive strain injury), and more.

Some very practical things you can do to help alleviate harmful effects of computer screens are keeping them turned off when not in use, using ra-

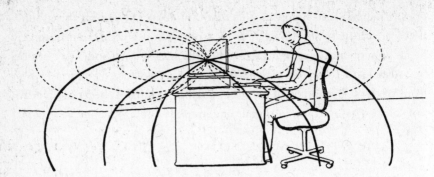

Magnetic (---) and electric (—) fields of a computer

diation screens, wearing natural fibers such as cotton rather than synthetics, and always having plants near computer equipment. While cacti are not ideal in terms of general Feng Shui principles because their sharp points produce nervous discomfort, the *Cereus Peruvianus* cactus has been found to be very effective in neutralizing the harmful effects of computer screens and has been introduced to the New York Stock Exchange for that purpose. Other plants you can use are listed later in this chapter.

Another solution is to switch to a laptop with an LCD (liquid crystal display) screen, which is a huge improvement on the cathode ray tube of conventional monitors. They emit far lower EMFs, and workers report huge increases in vitality and productivity after switching to one of these. This whole book was produced on a laptop. I find working on a cathode ray tube monitor totally debilitating.

A word of caution about laptops, however: do not work with one on your lap! You will actually soak up more radiation than working with a conventional screen if it is in direct contact with your physical body.

CELLULAR PHONES

Cellular phones work on microwave frequencies. Some of the radiation emitted by these phones is absorbed directly into the head of the user, and there is growing concern that regular use can cause or increase the likelihood of headaches, migraines, ear and eye problems, and even brain tumors. A number of claims for compensation have been made in the United States by executives who use mobile phones a lot and who have developed ear or brain tumors. The U.S. Food and Drug Administration has now advised people to use mobile phones only when necessary and to make the calls as brief as possible. Technology has now developed a global cellular telephone system, which transmits directly to low-orbit satellites rather than to nearby ground stations. This enables you to call anywhere in the world from a mobile phone, but beware because the emissions are correspondingly more powerful.

At the time of writing, a number of different types of shields are being developed that can be fitted to mobile phones to reduce the amount of radiation absorbed by the user. Until these are commercially available, if you must use a mobile phone, use it as little as possible or use a speaker phone rather than a handheld model.

BEEPERS AND PAGERS

In his book *Electromagnetic Pollution Solutions*, Dr. Glen Swartwout tells the story of a physician in Oregon who had chronic inflammation of his left foot. No treatment helped to relieve the condition. Eventually it was realized that he was wearing a beeper on the left side of his body on exactly the same meridian as the problem area of the foot. When he stopped wearing the beeper, the condition cleared. If you use a beeper or a pager, carry it in your bag rather than having it in contact with your body, and if you decide you absolutely must keep it on your person, then at least vary where you wear it.

MICROWAVE OVENS

Microwave ovens are now common in private homes and restaurants. When you microwave your food, the nitrogen bonds in proteins break. Some health experts believe that the food then becomes denatured and unrecognizable to your digestive system, but health risks have not yet been proven to the satisfaction of the authorities. They do agree, however, that microwave ovens may begin to leak microwaves with age, so regular checking is recommended.

Cooking is best done on an open fire; the next best alternative is gas. If you ever get the chance, try the experiment of cooking the same food on an open fire, an electric burner, a gas burner, and in a microwave oven. You will be amazed at how different the same food tastes when it is cooked by different methods.

PERSONAL APPLIANCES

It is much better to use rechargeable battery razors or good, old-fashioned, handheld razors rather than expose yourself to the high EMFs generated by electric razors. Hairdryers also have very high EMFs. I find that hairdryers really confuse my energy systems, and I always prefer to let my hair dry naturally. Hair stays in better condition that way too.

SYNTHETIC CLOTHING AND BEDDING

Synthetic clothing and bedding generate static electricity that can interfere with the delicate electromagnetic balances of the body's energy systems.

JEWELRY

Jewelry picks up specific frequencies from the atmosphere and transmits them directly to the body through the skin. Acupoints such as the earlobes and fingers (which is where jewelry is often worn) are especially conductive, and the effect of EMFs is therefore amplified. Many necklaces block the normal transmission of the electrical heart rhythm to the head, and they can interfere with the functions of the thymus and the meridians that pass through the neck. Costume jewelry made from alloys can also produce allergic reactions due to toxicity. Jewelry made of pure metals such as silver, gold, and platinum can be used selectively to enhance your energy for specific development purposes (see Chapter 6).

LIGHTING

The quality of lighting that we expose our bodies to is just as important as the quality of the air that we breathe or the water that we drink. Our bodies take in the nourishment of light through our skin (sunlight, for example, is the only way we can obtain vitamin D).

Most people intuitively feel that fluorescent lighting is bad for them without knowing why. Fluorescent tubes actually emit the same type of radiation as cathode ray tube computer monitors. Other hazards include flicker and glare, and low levels of microwave radiation. These can cause eye and skin irritations, sinus problems, nausea, hypertension, and violent behavioral changes, especially noticeable in children. Toxins such as phosphor (used to coat the inside of the glass tube) and mercury vapor are also found in fluorescent tubes. Reading this list makes you wonder why anyone ever uses them. The answer, of course, is that fluorescent lighting is so much cheaper to install and run than ordinary incandescent bulbs that employers allow themselves to be governed by economics rather than considering their workers' health.

Natural daylight is undoubtedly the best lighting of all. The next best option is full-spectrum lighting, which has shown remarkable results when installed to replace fluorescent lighting in schools. Studies in Canada and the United States have shown that violent behavior disappeared within weeks, former "problem" children turned out to be model pupils, and academic achievements and attendance improved. Unfortunately, many education authorities are unaware of these studies and continue to install fluorescent lighting in schools as a matter of course.

NEGATIVE IONIZATION

Pollution from car exhausts, air conditioning, cigarette smoking, fluorescent lighting, electrical, electronic, and microwave equipment, static-producing artificial fibers in carpets, curtains, clothes, and so on all reduce the level of negative ions in the atmosphere and increase the level of positive ions. If you wonder why you are more irritable and aggressive in towns than in the countryside, it is very probably due to the higher levels of positive ions in urban atmospheres.

In nature, the ratio of negative ions is higher on top of mountains, in parks and open spaces, by waterfalls, by fast-flowing streams, and by the sea. This accounts for why we all feel so much better in these types of places. Negative ions are generated by ultraviolet light from the sun, by water-droplet formation and by plants.

In another book by Roger Coghill, *Electrohealing*, he explains that "in a rural location one might find at least 1000 neg-ions per cubic centimeter, in a city there might be only 300 per cubic cm, and in an office as little as 50 neg-ions per cubic cm." A negative ionizer can help to restore the balance in your home providing you choose one that is properly insulated. Most ionizers are not and produce high electromagnetic fields, which make them therefore counterproductive. The only ionizers I have come across that are shielded are those made by Mountain Breeze.

AIR CLEANSING

Many of us spend much of our indoor lives breathing in chemical cocktails of mind-boggling complexity. Plastics, synthetic fibers, solvents, adhesives, household cleaners, hair sprays, cosmetics, and decorating materials all mingle together and create health hazards in poorly ventilated areas.

The chemical preservative formaldehyde is one of the main pollutants of our indoor environments and is known to cause eye, nose, and throat irritation, as well as headaches, nausea, disturbed sleep, and a host of other symptoms. It is found in many decorating materials, including carpets, paints, wallpapers, veneers, wood varnishes, adhesives, noniron and flame-resistant fabrics, foam rubbers, chipboard, and plywood, all of which continue to give off fumes for years.

We can benefit from research funded by NASA to discover ways of cleansing the air in space capsules. They discovered in the course of this research that several ordinary types of houseplants have the ability to cleanse many of the most common pollutants from the air, including formaldehyde. They are:

Peace lilies
(Spathiphyllum Wallisii)

Peperomias

Goosefoot plants
(Syngonium Podophyllum)

Dwarf banana plants

Golden Pothos
(Scindapsus Aureus)

Peace lily

Three other types of plants were found to perform the same function, but they are not so good to use in confined areas because their leaves are longer and spikier (see Chapter 19 for Feng Shui information about spiky plants). They are:

Chinese evergreens (Aglaonema)

Spider plants (Chlorophytum Elatum)

Mother-in-law's tongue (Sansevieria Trifasciata Laurentii)

As well as filtering the air, plants increase the oxygen content, improve humidity and negative ionization, and generally lift the energy of a space. My usual recommendation is one plant per computer or television, placed as near as possible to the equipment, and other plants as necessary to compensate for other electrical apparatus.

PART FIVE

Your Home As a Magical Manifesting Machine

16.

Feng Shui:
The Ancient Art
of Placement

Having cleared and consecrated your space and run checks for geopathic and electromagnetic stress, you are now in a prime position to begin working with the branch of Feng Shui that is best known in the West. This part of the book is a "window" into the ancient Chinese Feng Shui art of placement, a complex and fascinating subject that will cause you to look at buildings in a whole new way. I say it is a "window" because these chapters offer a succinct but only introductory glimpse of the scope of this art. There are many other books about classical Feng Shui placement, and I have recommended some in the Bibliography for those of you who will want to take the study further.

Space Clearing can be used independently of Feng Shui placement, and Feng Shui placement can be used independently of Space Clearing, but I find a blend of the two together consistently brings the best results.

HOW TO USE
FENG SHUI PLACEMENT

Whenever I move to a new home, the first thing I do after Space Clearing is to put in place any Feng Shui cures needed to compensate for poor design and then arrange my furniture and other Feng Shui enhancements according to the focus in my life at that time. I think of my home as a magical manifesting machine, the interface between myself and the universe. As I live my life, my home is constantly being updated and changed. I listen to my Higher Self, configure my home accordingly, and the frequencies ripple out into the cosmos and back again, bringing with them information about the next stage of my journey.

The Feng Shui art of placement is a wonderful tool that you can use to help you manifest the life you want. By consciously placing your desires and intention in your physical environment, your surroundings can support you in remarkable ways. This book is not about getting clear on what you want (there are many other books and teachers to help you with this), but this is a very, very important part of the process. Clarify your own intentions and represent them symbolically in your surroundings. Feng Shui enhancements such as furniture positioning, mirrors, and crystals can then be used to enhance the energy flow.

Some people are attracted to the use of Feng Shui as a get-rich-quick technique. They hear that you can hang a crystal in your "wealth" corner and sit back and watch the money roll in. Of course it is not actually so simple. If you have already done a lot of personal work and your home environment is energetically clear, it can be like that, but for most people there is a whole process of aligning themselves to the flow of universal abundance, which must be gone through in stages. The beauty of Feng Shui is that when you make changes in your external environment, they are tangible and visible. You can see what is happening internally by the changes you make externally. Many people find this way of changing so much easier than battling with inner issues through deep introspective therapies.

Feng Shui placement extends into many aspects of a home. A building's overall shape and the internal layout of rooms are very important, and Feng Shui gives guidelines for the positioning of doors, windows, beds, desks, stoves, baths, toilets, fireplaces, and other key structures in order to enhance the energy flow and create harmony in your life.

Preventative versus curative Feng Shui

Feng Shui in the East is generally of the preventative variety, whereas most of my work in the West is curative Feng Shui. I am called in to identify and correct design faults that are producing adverse effects. A small percentage of places (often houses converted into apartments) are so awful that they are untreatable, but in most cases there are simple solutions that can be implemented.

FENG SHUI:
THE LANGUAGE OF SYMBOLOGY

Everything has a symbology and an effect. Take as an example the red triangle, which is used to border warning road signs throughout the world. The shape and color of a red triangle is a symbol universally recognized by the subconscious mind as meaning there is danger. Some kinds of symbology in people's homes have similar universal significance, and some may have significance only to them because they relate to particular events in their pasts.

Take a fresh look at your pictures and household decorations. Are they symbolic of what you want them to be? Begin now to consciously create your environment. If you want to be more spiritual in your life, surround yourself with objects that stimulate your spirituality. If you want more friends, have groups of decorative objects and group photos around your home rather than single objects and images. For more prosperity, create the symbolism of abundance in your space. If your life feels drab and dull, bring in some colorful decorations to liven things up. For more movement in your life, replace still-life pictures with activity scenes. For more ease and flow, replace geometric patterns and hard lines with smooth flowing shapes.

Always look to see what message your pictures and decorations are giving out. As an example, I often find that unhappy single people have a picture of a tragic-looking solitary person in a prime position in their home. Usually they are very attracted to this picture and no matter how much they want their life to change, they are not willing to get rid of it. If this is the case, my tactic is generally to suggest they take it down for a while and replace it with a picture that lifts their spirits whenever they see it. By doing this, they come to realize themselves what an effect the old picture was having on them.

If your life is not going too well and hasn't been for some time, this will be reflected in the symbology of things around your home, and something I have noticed again and again in the homes of people who feel hopeless or depressed is that they have lots of hanging things.

Let me describe the home of one such woman I visited. In her kitchen, all the cups and pans were hanging from hooks, together with keys and other miscellaneous objects. In her bedroom there were clothes and bags hanging from hooks and doorknobs, and she had even created a way of stringing her earrings between two poles on her dressing table (needless to say, all her earrings were drop earrings!). She had spider plants and other trailing plants hanging from baskets all over the house. All her lampshades angled the light down rather than up, and all the ceilings were very low, which pulled the energy down even more. There were probably over a hundred hanging objects in her small home. The whole effect was very depressing, and it was clear to me that she must be very depressed to have created such symbolism around her.

I recommended that she simply go around her home and reverse the direction of every hanging object so that the energy would naturally move upward rather than downward. I suggested she stack her pans rather than hang them, put her cups on shelves, train her trailing plants to become climbers, replace her downlighting with uplighting, and so on. The results of this were remarkable. To put it in her own words, "I hadn't realized it, but even my head was hanging down as I walked. Now I walk tall and feel glad to be alive!"

Incidentally, spider plants are a great favorite with people who feel depressed. They droop and trail and produce little baby spider plants all over the place, which symbolically multiplies the person's problems! Their leaves are also spiky, which can produce anxiety and agitation. Some people keep spider plants because they have heard they are good for cleansing the air, but they function at very low levels of energy, and too many of them in a space will pull the atmosphere down. There are other plants that will cleanse the air just as well without any of these other side effects (see Chapter 15). It's fine to have one or two small spider plants around your home, but don't let them take over!

CUTTING CHI

The whole of Feng Shui is based on the principle of creating ease and harmony in your home to create ease and harmony in your life, so the symbolism of flowing curves and patterns is better than geometric angles (there are, after all, no straight lines in nature). Sharp corners and pointed objects produce disruption and disharmony because they emanate invisible rays.

Cutting chi of furniture

Take the example of a reception area in a home or an office where there is a sharp corner of a cupboard, shelf, or desk pointing toward your stomach as you enter. You may not notice the effect consciously, but your body will be very aware of it and will avoid being directly in line with the point if space permits. Visitors will feel less welcome, and anyone walking through this area many times a day may even develop stomach problems.

To get firsthand experience of this, roll up your sleeves, take off your watch and any jewelry you are wearing on your hands or wrists, wash your hands, and go through the exercise to sensitize your hands in Chapter 6 (if you are already familiar with this, just use your link signal). Find a piece of furniture with sharp corners or two walls that form a point projecting outward, and approach it from a few feet away, sensing the point with your hands. As you move closer, the sensations will intensify. Most people are amazed the first time they feel this. Even after you draw your hand away, you can still feel a dull ache in the palm of your hand. In the

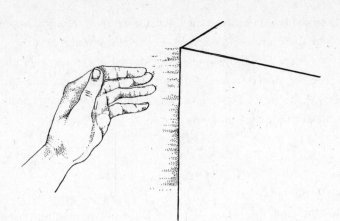

Sensing cutting chi with the hand

following chapter, I explain the potential hazards of cutting chi in relation to bedroom furniture and light fixtures.

To alleviate the kind of cutting chi described in the reception area, move the furniture to a less intrusive position or have the points rounded off. Another solution is to drape a cloth or a round-leafed trailing plant over the sharp edges, or place an upward-shooting, round-leafed potted plant in front of the point. Better still, choose furniture with rounded edges in the first place so you won't have this problem at all.

Cutting chi from outside the home

A similar problem can occur on a grander scale if the corner of a neighboring building points directly at your front door or one of your windows. A tree, hedge, or large bush planted between your home and the source of the corner of the offending building may alleviate the effects, or a mirror placed facing out of your window, reflecting the corner back to itself is a Feng Shui cure often used.

Another form of cutting chi that can have a penetrating effect on your life is if your home is situated at the top of a T-junction, especially if your front door is directly in line with the road opposite.

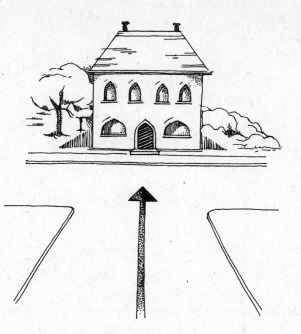

Cutting chi at a T-junction

In this location, arrowlike energy is coming toward you as cars come down the road. The detrimental effect is relative to the size of your house, the size of the road, and the speed of the cars (if you have a big house and the road opposite is a tiny backroad which hardly anyone uses, the effect is negligible). A brass plate, spherical door pull, or other reflective device can be placed on the front door to deflect this type of cutting chi. Another solution is to move the path to your front door a few feet to one side so that the path curves toward the door from a different angle than the approaching road. Then plant a hedge between your door and the road.

Having explained these fundamental principles, let's take a look now at some key aspects of the interior layout of your home.

17

Move Your Sofa
and Change
Your Life!

When you hear of wonderful changes happening in people's lives because a Feng Shui consultant has told them to move their sofa, the likelihood is that the sofa was blocking the main thoroughfare through their home and therefore blocking incoming energy. This chapter is about maximizing the flow of energy around your home to make it easier to manifest your ideal life.

DOORS

Your front entrance

I always pay particular attention to the front entrance of a home. Just as people enter and leave through the main front door, so it is also the portal through which energy flows into and out of a person's life. As you come into your home, what you see and experience represents your approach to your own life, and as you leave your home, it represents your approach to the outer world.

Next time you stand outside the front entrance to your home, look at it with fresh eyes. If you did not know who lived here, what could you deduce from looking at this front door? Is the paint peeling? Is the doorbell broken? Is the path overgrown?

If you have to battle through overhanging branches, trailing plants, spiky hedges, or other assorted debris to get into or out of your home, it will feel like you have to struggle to achieve anything in life. Keep your front path as clear as possible. It is also important that the front entrance is welcoming, so that you feel glad to arrive home. A fresh new coat of paint, flowering plants in pots positioned on either side of the front door, hanging baskets, and window boxes are all ways to brighten up the front area.

If you have a number on your front door, position it high up rather than low down (looking down causes your energy to drop), and if you live in a house with two or more numbers in its address, here's a lovely Feng Shui tip: position the second and subsequent numbers so that they are slightly higher than the first number. This will give you an energy lift every time you walk in your front door. You can apply the same principles to lettering if your house has a name rather than a number.

Your life will work easiest if your front door opens inward flat against the wall, unobstructed by clutter. A front door that sticks means things won't go as smoothly for you as they could, and if you have to jiggle the key every time to make it work, your life will be full of small irritations. Keeping your front door in good repair will ensure that energy can move more easily into your life.

If you come face to face with a brick wall as soon as you come through your front door, you will understand what the old saying, "coming up against a brick wall" is all about. Over a period of time this can engender feelings of defeat and hopelessness. Eventually it may even affect your posture, causing your shoulders to droop and hunch forward. Hang a mirror on the wall to bring depth into the space, or at least a picture that inspires you. If the area immediately inside the front door is dingy, install lighting.

Internal doors

Something I have noticed about people who have a lot of struggle in their lives and who tend to feel stuck is that they have cumbersome structures in their homes that they have to maneuver around. One typical example is if they have many interior doors that open awkwardly into a wall rather than opening flat against the wall. In other words, the way the doors are hung means that you enter by walking toward the wall inside the doorway rather than straight into the rooms, and you cannot see the rooms until the doors have been pushed fully open. This makes it really difficult for energy to flow easily around a home.

As well as causing stuckness on a mental and emotional level, if you live for a long time in a house with lots of doors like this, you will also tend to be physically constipated! In England, all houses built in Victorian times were designed with doors opening this way, in order to preserve privacy. Something the history books have failed to record is that Victorian England must have been a land of very constipated people!

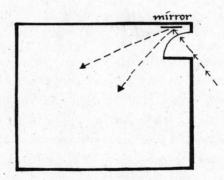

Cure for an awkwardly opening door

One solution to this design problem is to rehang all your doors, and it feels wonderful if you do it. Everything feels so much easier in every aspect of your life. Another solution is to hang a small mirror just inside the door, to redirect energy into the room. First read the guidelines for hanging mirrors in Chapter 19. Also take care when hanging mirrors near light switches that you don't inadvertently bash a nail through an electrical cable, or you may get more energy than you bargained for! If in doubt, consult a qualified electrician.

Another way to improve the flow of energy in your life is to make sure that all your internal doors can open fully and are not obstructed by clutter or items of furniture. Clothing hanging on hooks behind doors can prevent the door from opening to the widest extent of its arc and will increase the weight of the door, again adding more struggle to your life.

W I N D O W S

Windows are the "eyes" of your home. Cracked panes can literally affect the way you view life and may even create eye problems. If your windows are grimy, your vision of life and your insights into what is happening in your life will be restricted. It will be as if you cannot see past your own little world, past your own fixed views.

Clean your windows and bring greater clarity and vision into your life. Windows that only open partially (such as sash windows) can have the effect of limiting you. The best windows to have are the hinged kind that open fully outward and admit the maximum possible energy into your life.

B E D R O O M S   A N D   B E D S

The siting of bedrooms and positioning of beds has always been considered of major importance in Feng Shui traditions of every culture.

Siting bedrooms

Check for geopathic and electromagnetic stress before deciding which rooms will be used as bedrooms and where beds can be placed in those rooms (see Chapters 14 and 15). It is generally best to site bedrooms as far away from the front entrance as possible, especially the master bedroom. When you sleep in this position you have the sense that you can see things coming in your life and have time to consider your options and decide what is the best thing to do. If you sleep too close to the front door, things happen suddenly and take you by surprise, so you may miss opportunities and make choices you regret. You can expect to experience greater feelings of inner peace sleeping in this position. When you feel more secure during your hours of sleep, you naturally feel more secure as you go about your life. It therefore becomes much easier to manifest what you want to have happen in your life.

Positioning your bed

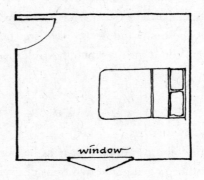

Ideally placed bed

Where you place your bed within the bedroom is also important. If your bed is too close to the bedroom door, you will never completely relax while

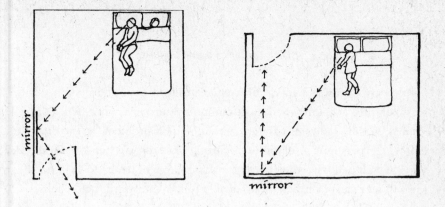

Positioning of mirror to give a view of the door from a bed

you sleep. A part of you will always stay on alert for someone coming into the room, even if you live alone. Similarly, if you position your bed with a window behind your head you will always be listening for intruders coming up from behind, which can create stress and feelings of vulnerability.

The best place to have your bed is as far away from the door as possible, ideally square onto the wall and diagonally opposite to the door (close to the wall but not right up to it), with a clear view of the door and windows. If this is impossible, you can do clever things with mirrors to ensure that you still have a view of the door. Have a look at the diagrams above.

Never place your bed so that your feet are pointing toward the door. This is called the "coffin position," because traditionally they carry out the dead feet first. Some English hospital regulations state that patients' beds are never to be wheeled feet first through a doorway, because it is recognized that this has a detrimental effect on a patient's health and well-being. The connection between "feet first" and death is deeply embedded in our psyche.

If there is absolutely no alternative to sleeping in this position, fit a footboard to create a shield between you and the door. A makeshift alternative would be positioning a small chest of drawers between the end of the bed and the door.

Bedroom furniture

Cutting chi (arrowlike energy that emanates from sharp corners) needs to be taken into account when positioning furniture near your bed. Square-shaped bedside tables or cabinets are a common problem. In the diagram below, the person is sleeping with cutting chi crossing him in two directions, which will have the effect of making him feel hemmed in in his life. He will feel inexplicably limited, unable to move forward, held back.

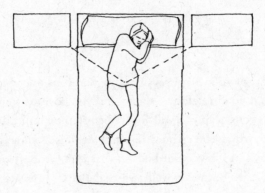

Cutting chi from bedside cupboards

Where larger pieces of furniture are aiming cutting chi at the sleeping place, the person will feel as if unseen forces are ready to act if he moves forward (see the diagram on the opposite page).

The effects of cutting chi diminish with distance, so positioning furniture farther away from the bed is one solution if space permits. Bedside tables can be softened by draping soft cloths over the corners or, better still, replacing the tables with rounded ones.

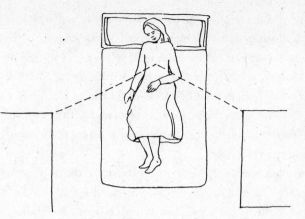

Cutting chi from bedside furniture

Beds

It is best to sleep on a wooden bed, with a mattress made from natural fibers, as described in Chapter 14. Have your bed raised a little off the ground so that air can circulate underneath it.

Beds become energetically saturated over a period of time because people discharge energy during sleep. I recommend that you change your bed every time you make a major change in your life, or certainly at least every ten years. If you are starting a new relationship or moving to a new home, that is also an excellent time to treat yourself to a new bed. If this is impractical, at least consider treating yourself to new sheets. It is unwise to sleep with a new partner in the bed you shared for a long time with a lover from a failed relationship!

If you want intimacy with your partner, never choose a bed with a split down the middle, and if you check into a hotel for a romantic getaway, never accept a room where you are expected to sleep on twin beds pushed together to make a double bed. On a deep subconscious level, sleeping in a split bed produces the feeling of there being an irreconcilable gap between you!

Also beware of positioning your bed beneath an exposed beam. A lengthwise beam running down the middle of a bed can wreck a good marriage, and a crosswise beam can result in medical problems in whatever part of the body it crosses. Criss-crossing beams in a bedroom are a Feng Shui nightmare. Usually it helps to blunt any sharp edges on the beams and paint them the same color as the ceiling so that they appear to recede into it rather than protrude from it. The best solution is to install a false ceiling to cover them or move your bed to another room. If none of these options are possible, I consider the problems associated with beams so harmful that I usually recommend moving, especially if marital or health difficulties have already developed.

Apart from beams, it is best not to have anything hanging down from the ceiling over the bed either. Many is the time I have gone to do a consultation in someone's home and found a fiendish-looking light fixture hanging over someone's sleeping space that is creating medical problems for him or her. By looking at the position of the fixture in relation to where the person's body would be in the bed, I can tell where in the body the person is having problems.

The worst kind of lampshades or fixtures are those with sharp downward points. In one client's bedroom there was a large, ugly light fixture with seven downward points hanging right over the area of her womb as she lay in the bed. When she told me she had been sleeping there for three years, I knew she was heading for a hysterectomy if she hadn't already had one. It turned out she had had one two years previously and was still experiencing problems in that area of her body. I advised her to move her bed, and she called me a couple of weeks later to let me know that she no longer had any pain at night. A year later the condition had cleared completely.

This is only one of many, many examples I see as I go about my work. If you must have your bed under a light fixture because there is nowhere else to put it, choose a rounded or globe-shaped lampshade, which is far kinder to your body.

OFFICES AND DESKS

When I tell my Balinese friends that people in the West sit in offices with their desks facing the wall and their backs to each other, they dissolve in fits of laughter! They say it explains why so many Western people have glassy stares!

Feng Shui rules for positioning desks very closely follow those for beds. First check for geopathic and electromagnetic stress. The ideal position for a desk is diagonally opposite the door with your back squarely to the wall, in such a way that you have a clear view of the door and any windows. This will place you in the power point of the room and will offer you the greatest creative possibility and also the greatest feeling of security and control. If the design of the space permits, it is wonderful to place your desk in the Fortunate Blessings area of the room.

Avoid having your desk directly in line with the door or sitting with your back to a window, because these factors will weaken your position. Never sit with your back to the door when you are working. Part of your awareness will always be tied up in sensing whether someone has come up behind you, and your nerves, productivity, and efficiency will all suffer as a result. If sitting in this position is unavoidable, a Feng Shui cure is to hang a mirror above the desk to reflect people approaching you from behind.

If you work at home, position your desk so that as you work you are facing toward your home rather than away from it. This will allow you and your family to feel that you are still included in family life as you do your work, and you can keep the energy flowing between you. When you turn your back to your family as you work, the message you send out is that you are closed to them at that time, which means you deprive yourself and them.

Desks in offices are best turned to face toward each other, taking into account as many of the factors I have already mentioned as possible. When I do business consultations I always prefer a time when the office is empty of staff. Just by going around and looking at the positions of desks and a few other salient features, I am able to give the owner a complete profile of each employee, how they relate to the employer and each other, what their personal strengths and weaknesses, talents and struggles are, and which of them are thinking of leaving. The potential leavers generally have their desks positioned with their backs to the door or in some other awkward kind of position.

One of my clients was the owner of a firm of tour operators who had sat for years at the rear of his open plan office with his face to the wall and his back to his staff and to the front entrance. After a Feng Shui consultation he turned the desk around and moved the stack of filing cabinets in the middle of the office which had blocked access to him. A month later a contract appeared out of nowhere, and his company is now the number one tour operator in Cuba. Business became so busy that six months later he still had not had the opportunity to print any brochures for the tours, but they were selling like hotcakes nevertheless!

18.

The Bagua

A wonderful tool developed by one of the Chinese systems of Feng Shui is a grid called the bagua. It derives from the *I Ching (The Chinese Book of Changes)* and can be laid over the plans of your home or workplace to show which areas of the building relate to which aspects of your life. Knowing this means that everything in your home takes on even more significance, because now its symbolism can be directly related to different aspects of your life. As I so often say to clients when they are pleading the case for keeping some bedraggled spiky-leafed plant in their Relationships area—is that what you *want* your relationship life to look like?

Just as life is a series of microcosms within macrocosms, so there are baguas within baguas. There is a bagua of the plot of land that your home stands on. Then there is a bagua for the actual building. Within that there are baguas for each room within the building. You can even take it right down to the baguas of individual desks, beds, and so on.

USING THE BAGUA

Draw a rough sketch of the plans of your home on a piece of paper, as much to scale as possible and showing the different rooms. If you live in a house with several stories, for now just draw the story where you normally

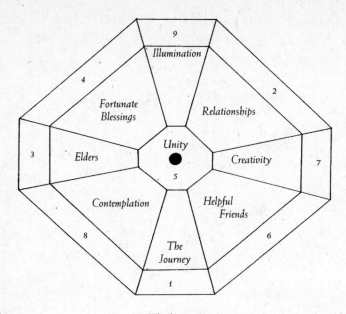

The bagua

enter your home. Now reproduce the octagonal bagua grid on a piece of tracing paper or other transparent material. If your home is a perfect square, rectangle, or other symmetrical shape, draw two diagonal lines faintly in pencil as shown in these diagrams:

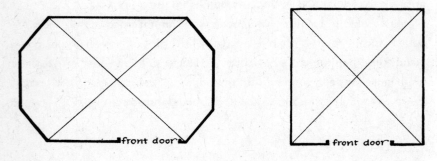

Symmetrical shapes

If your home is an irregular shape, you will need to square it off before you can draw these lines in. Look at the following examples:

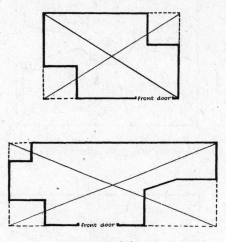

Asymmetrical shapes

Now place the center point of the bagua grid over the exact point where the two diagonal lines intersect. The bagua has an elastic quality, so you can extend or contract the lines to stretch or shrink to whatever shape your home is.

Finally, swivel the bagua so that its lower edge is aligned with the door through which people (and energy) come into your home. For most people this will be their front door, but it may be a side door or a back door if that is what everyone always uses. If you live in an apartment within a house or you just rent a room within a house, simply take the main door of your apartment or room as being the entrance to which you align the bagua. Here are some examples of different-shaped homes and how to align the bagua grid.

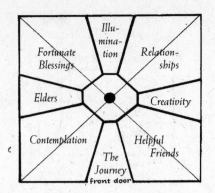

Aligning the bagua—symmetrical shape

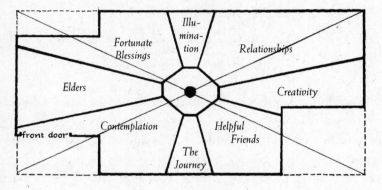

Aligning the bagua—assymmetrical shape

If your home has more than one story, each floor has its own bagua, and in most buildings the bagua will be aligned in different directions on different stories. Simply align the lower edge of the bagua with the direction you face as your staircase arrives on that level.

Missing areas (negative space)

If your home is a square, rectangle, or other symmetrical shape, the complete bagua will be represented. If, however, it is irregularly shaped, one or more areas of the bagua may be missing, and this can create challenges in the corresponding area(s) of your life. Many people find that their lives take a downhill turn after erecting an extension across part of the back of their home, thus creating a missing area, or that their lives improve after adding a new room to square off the missing area.

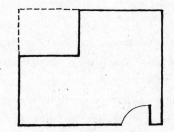

Missing Fortunate Blessings area

After explaining the nine areas of the bagua, I will go through each of the Feng Shui cures that can be used to bring in missing areas and also explain how Feng Shui adjustments can be used to enhance different aspects of your life.

THE NINE AREAS OF THE BAGUA

Read through the following descriptions and then decide which area or areas you would like to focus on. It works best to begin with just one area, or two at the most.

    The names given in brackets are those traditionally used to describe the different areas. In his excellent book *Feng Shui Made Easy*, William Spear has updated these names to convey more deeply the essence of each aspect and has kindly given his permission for me to use these names here.

1. *The Journey (also known as Career)*

This area represents not only what you do to earn money on a material level but also your path in life on a more spiritual level, and the way that you approach things generally. It has to do with new beginnings and opportunities. Use Feng Shui enhancements in this area to improve career prospects, help you find your direction in life, and create ease and flow.

2. *Relationships (also known as Marriage)*

The Relationships area concerns your primary relationship with your sexual partner, as well as your relationship with yourself, your family, friends, colleagues, and people and things in general. If you are single and looking for a partner, this is the area of your home to augment. If you are already married, Feng Shui enhancements here will help to keep your relationship energized and vital. They can also bring more harmony and positivity into the way you interact with everyone you know.

3. *Elders (also known as Family)*

This area relates to your heritage, ancestors, parents, superiors, and influences from the past. It is the foundation from which you operate, either consciously or unconsciously. By clearing clutter and enhancing this area of your home, you make a significant contribution to improving your relationship with your parents and all authority figures.

4. *Fortunate Blessings (also known as Wealth or Prosperity)*

The Fortunate Blessings area of a home has to do with the flow of universal abundance into your life. It can take the form of material possessions and money, and also blessings and prosperity in all its many other forms. Many people choose to boost the Feng Shui of this area to increase their affluence, and this is obviously of key importance to businesses. If your toilet, junk room, or garbage area are situated in your Fortunate Blessings area, your prosperity could suffer.

5. *Unity (also known as Tai Chi or Health)*

Just as good health is central to our happiness and enjoyment of life, so the area connected to health and vitality is to be found at the center of a building. If this area of your home is cluttered you are likely to experience tiredness and fatigue, so keep it as clear as possible. The Chinese traditionally built their homes with a courtyard at the center so that this area was unoccupied. If you have chronic health problems, also check that the center of each of your rooms is clear.

6. *Helpful Friends (also known as Helpful People)*

It's amazing how many offers of help come pouring in when you boost the Feng Shui in the Helpful Friends area of your home. It may be help from family, friends, colleagues, officials, people you've never met before, or even just opening a book at the right page and finding an answer you've been looking for. This is a wonderful place to site an altar in your home, where you can leave petitions to God, the universe, angels, guides, unseen helpers, and so on. Since you receive back according to what you give out, this area is also associated with your own philanthropic acts.

7. Creativity (also known as Offspring)

This part of the bagua concerns anything you create or give birth to in the world. Augment this area to nurture your children and projects to maturity. This is also an excellent place to put a "treasure map," a pictorial representation of something you want to manifest in your life such as a new car, a better job, or a trip somewhere you've always wanted to go. I know many wonderful stories of results produced in this way in my own life and in those of others. Be sure to put a happy, smiling photo of you in the picture.

8. Contemplation (also known as Inner Knowledge)

This area is associated with new learning, introspection, meditation, and inner guidance. It is an ideal place in a home to site a library, a study, or meditation room. Enhance this area if you want to improve your studying, intuition, spiritual focus, or guidance from your Higher Self.

9. Illumination (also known as Fame)

Each person is unique. This area has to do with the expression of your individuality, what lights you up in your life, and what you are known for. On a higher level it concerns spiritual enlightenment and self-realization. This is the area to boost if you want to develop your charisma, have greater clarity in your life, enhance your reputation in the world, and/or develop your spiritual potential. Because it is on the opposite wall to the door, this area is often the focal point of a room.

WHAT TO DO IF YOUR TOILET IS INAUSPICIOUSLY SITUATED

For most westerners, the auspicious positioning of their toilet is a concern that would never have entered their heads. But for anyone with knowledge of the bagua this is a very important consideration. Over the centuries Feng Shui practitioners have discovered that if a toilet is situated in the Fortunate Blessings area of a home, it can create problems with prosperity. It is as if you are symbolically flushing your profits down the toilet! You may have money coming in, but with your toilet in this position you will have just as much going out. In 1993, when interest in Feng Shui was in its early stages in the United Kingdom, I appeared on Granada TV's *This Morning* program and explained about the problems caused by having a toilet in this area of a home. The public response took Granada's switchboard by surprise—a deluge of phone calls from people saying, "That explains why we've been losing money ever since we moved to this house!"

There are, fortunately, a number of Feng Shui solutions to this problem, and they work best if all are implemented simultaneously.

1. If there is a window in the room, hang a spherical multi-faceted rainbow crystal there so that it brings as much rainbow light into the room as possible.
2. Keep the toilet seat down when the toilet is not in use.
3. If the toilet is in a separate room from the bathroom, keep the toilet door closed and put a mirror on the outside of the door to deflect energy away. The mirror can be of any size, providing it is framed and hung securely flat against the surface of the door (see the following chapter for further information about hanging mirrors).
4. Put a healthy, round-leafed, upward-shooting plant in the room to energize the space or, if this is not possible, a picture of a prolific-looking tree or plant, or some flowers in bloom.

These cures do resolve the problem in most cases, but just as you will always have to take care to keep the door closed and the toilet seat down while you live in a home with a toilet in this position, so you will always have to be careful about money for as long as you live there. When looking for a new home in the future you may be able to save yourself some legwork by asking the real-estate agents if a floor plan is available for you to look at first to check the position of the toilet.

19.

More
Feng Shui Magic

Before describing some more of the ways Feng Shui can be used to bring magical transformations into your life, I have one very important piece of advice for you:

> Make Feng Shui changes SLOWLY
> AFTER clearing clutter.

Don't try to Feng Shui your whole house at once. Do it gradually. First, clear any clutter. If you make Feng Shui changes without bothering to do this, you can actually exacerbate your problems rather than relieve them. If you have not already Space Cleared your home, do this now. Then choose one or at most two areas of your life you would like to focus on. With each change you make in your home, integrate it and let the energy settle before making the next one.

One self-employed and very successful beautician who came to one of my workshops decided not to heed this advice. She went home and rushed around her house putting up mirrors and crystals and moving all her furniture. The next day, six clients phoned to cancel their appointments. Another woman did the same after a private consultation, until her family stepped in and announced they would all leave if she didn't slow down.

After reading the previous chapter and this one, you will feel energized and excited and eager to begin. Please contain yourself!

FENG SHUI CURES AND ENHANCEMENTS

Feng Shui cures are designed to correct the flow of energy in your home, whereas enhancements boost the energy of a particular aspect. For example, a home with a missing Fortunate Blessings area would require a permanent cure to correct the situation. In another home where the Fortunate Blessings area was present but the occupants' prosperity was flagging, a Feng Shui enhancement could be used for a while to revitalize the area. Remember that life is constantly shifting and changing. Your focus will change as you change and grow.

Remember also as you read this next section that each room within your home has its own bagua (place the center of the grid at the center of the room and turn it so that its lower edge is aligned to the entrance to the room). Therefore if you want to enhance a particular aspect of your life, augment the area in the greater bagua of your home and reinforce that in the corresponding area of the baguas of each room, especially the rooms where you spend the most time.

As with Space Clearing, the clearer you are about what you want to happen in your life, the more effective the Feng Shui cures and enhancements can be. They are even more profound when they are placed intentionally, with the heartfelt wish that the very best things happen for the highest good of everyone concerned. You may even choose to create a small ceremony as you install each Feng Shui adjustment to focus your intention and maximize its effectiveness.

MIRRORS

Deeply embedded in the subconscious mind of every Western person is the childhood story of Snow White and the Seven Dwarfs. Her wicked stepmother, the beautiful but vain queen, asks her mirror every day, "Mirror, mirror, on the wall, who is the fairest of them all?" The mirror always answers truthfully, no matter how enraged the queen becomes when it begins to tell her that Snow White is more beautiful than she is.

Then there are great literary works, such as Lewis Carroll's *Alice Through the Looking Glass*, and the age-old superstition that to break a mirror is seven years' bad luck. Mirrors have often been ascribed magical properties, and they are in fact incredibly powerful transmuters of energy. They have so many uses within the context of Feng Shui that they are often referred to as "the aspirin of Feng Shui," the all-purpose cure-all.

Mirrors as Feng Shui cures

Mirrors are one excellent way of correcting a missing area in a home. In the following illustration, the missing Fortunate Blessings area of this home is symbolically brought in by placing a mirror on either of the internal walls shown, with its reflective surface facing into the room. It is not necessary to place mirrors on both walls. (Note: If you have a window on one of these walls, you may prefer to use a crystal rather than a mirror—see page 229.)

Using mirrors in conjunction with the bagua

When you hang mirrors in areas of the bagua that you want to enhance, this is when you really start to appreciate how powerful they are. It's like turning up the volume in the energy worlds to bring much more of that vibration into your space. You can overdo it, of course. Too many mirrors

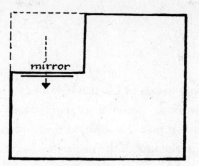

Mirror correcting a missing area

can be too much to handle and can make you feel giddy and nauseous. One mirror per room is fine, and other smaller mirrors can be added as required.

Mirrors to open up a space

Mirrors can be used to bring more light (and symbolically more positive energy) into gloomy areas such as dingy hallways. They can also be used to give the illusion of a small room being much larger. A perfect example of this can be found in toilets of commercial airlines, where the tiny cubicle would feel very claustrophobic without a mirror. Used frequently in restaurants and shops to create spaciousness, mirrors can also enlarge rooms and narrow passageways in homes.

Symbolic doubling with mirrors

You can use mirrors to symbolically double energy. A favorite Feng Shui tip for businesses is placing a mirror to reflect the cash register in order to double profits or placing mirrors behind products on shelves to double sales. A mirror reflecting a workdesk, on the other hand, is not such a good idea, because this symbolically doubles the workload without necessarily enhancing the returns! Be sure also to clear your clutter before hanging mirrors, otherwise you will only double your problems!

Mirrors in the bedroom

Lots of mirrors in your bedroom can make it difficult to get a good night's sleep. Rounded mirrors are better than angular ones for bedrooms, and never hang them so that you can see your own reflection from your bed. Mirrors at the head or the foot of the bed are also inadvisable. In children's bedrooms, have no mirrors at all unless the child wants one.

Storing mirrors

Because they are so powerful, it is not advisable to leave mirrors haphazardly leaning against walls, bouncing energy randomly around the place. This can create chaos and confusion in your life. If a mirror is not in use, deactivate it by covering it or laying it face down so that light is not reflected.

How to hang mirrors

Hang mirrors so that they do not reflect an image cutting off the top or bottom of the head of people who regularly see themselves in that mirror. If you have children, it is best to position mirrors so that they can either comfortably see themselves or not see themselves at all. If a child can only just see his or her eyes in a mirror, this can produce feelings of inadequacy and not being good enough.

If a mirror is positioned so that it only reflects part of the body below the head, this may produce a physical ailment at the level at which the mirror bisects the body. For example, if you have a mirror in your home in which you frequently see your reflection but it is from the waist down only, your body will feel bisected at waist level and may well develop a problem in that area. The main culprits for this kind of thing are long mirrors propped against walls instead of being hung, and dressing table mirrors in bedrooms.

One woman had a mirror that was hung too low for her to see the top of her head reflected in it, and she had been having blinding headaches for years. It was in the central area of her apartment, which meant that she saw herself with the top of her head cut off many times a day. When she re-hung the mirror high enough to see the whole of her head in it, her head-aches disappeared.

Hang the mirrors you look at yourself in most often so that your re-flection shows plenty of space above your head, which gives you room for expanding your higher possibilities.

Be particularly careful not to position mirrors so that they reflect one another. The energy will bounce back and forth between them, going nowhere fast. One man who had two mirrors opposite each other in a cor-ridor that was in the career area of his apartment was working very hard but making no progress in his career. As soon as he took one of the mirrors down, his work took off.

Also bear in mind that hanging a mirror in the most ideal position in the bagua will be of little use if the mirror itself reflects an image of some-thing unsightly. Always hang mirrors to reflect pleasing views.

Do not lean mirrors against the wall or tilt them at an angle. Slanted mirrors create results that are not quite what you wanted. Fix them securely to the wall.

What kinds of mirrors to use

For indoor purposes, generally the bigger the mirror the better, provided it is in proportion to the room. It is always best to use framed mirrors, unless the glass is cut to fit snugly into an alcove or recess. Raw edges on mirrors will produce raw edges in your life. Frames can be circular, oval, square, or rectangular.

Use mirrors that are wide enough so that you don't feel you have to constrict yourself physically to fit all of you in. This is particularly im-portant for full-length dressing mirrors. You will feel more powerful in your life if you see yourself reflected with room around you to expand into.

Mirror tiles are a real no-no. They break up your reflection into

dozens of tiny pieces and fragment your life accordingly. Larger tiled mirrors and mirror closets can also have undesirable effects.

Convex mirrors can be used to really pep up the energy when you
need it. They are a bit like antibiotics in the sense that if you use them in
cases of real emergency they work excellently, but if you take antibiotics
for every little ailment, then, when you really need them, they are only
minimally effective. They can also be counterproductive if used continually. One business client put a convex mirror in her Helpful Friends area
when she couldn't get any staff and received dozens of applications from
people wanting to work for her. She moved it to her Fortunate Blessings
area when finances took a downturn, and they quickly revived. She continues to use it as the occasion warrants.

Mirror maintenance

Keep your mirrors sparkling clean and they will serve you wonderfully. It
is best to use mirrors that have a good reflective surface. Tarnished mirrors
produce tarnished results, and worst of all are distressed antique mirrors.
One of my clients had a lovely big house with three enormous distressed
mirrors in the entrance foyer, which was in the career area of her house. It
turned out that since hanging the mirrors three years previously, neither
she nor her husband had had any work at all, and "distressed" certainly did
sum up the state of their financial affairs. Cracked mirrors need to be re-
paired or removed immediately.

CRYSTALS

How to use crystals

You can feel the uplifting effect when you walk into a room sparkling with
rainbow lights from a crystal hung in the window! The crystal is refracting
the light energy of the sun and dispersing it throughout the room. It is
symbolically bringing more positive life force into your home. Crystals fo-

cus, activate, and lift energy, and they work best if they are hung in windows receiving plenty of sunlight.

Crystals can be used to enhance a particular area of the bagua or as a cure for a missing area in your home. Hang one in the window looking out on to the missing space to symbolically bring its energy into your home.

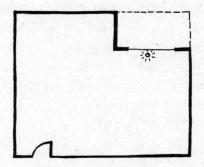

Crystal correcting a missing area

How to hang crystals

It generally works best to hang the crystal in the upper portion of a window in the center of the pane of glass. Because they activate the energy of whichever areas they are hung in, it is vital that whatever is close by is symbolic of what you want to have happen in your life!

What kind of crystals to use

Clear, multifaceted, leaded rainbow crystals are best. The full spectrum of rainbow colors means that you are invoking all possibilities in order to achieve your highest potential. Spherical crystals produce the most holistic effect, and they come in sizes ranging from one inch in diameter, suitable for smaller-sized rooms and for children's rooms, to a mega three or four inches in diameter, which is only recommended for banquet halls and the like! Choose the size that feels most appropriate for the window you wish to hang it in.

Looking after your crystals

Never use a crystal that is chipped. This can distort the energy and produce unwanted results. Always keep your windows and crystals sparkling clean. Wash your crystals as part of your weekly housekeeping routine, or at least make sure they are washed once a month. An easy way to remember is always to clean them on the first day of each month. You can wash them where they are hanging by dunking them in a small bowl of pure still spring water and leaving them to drip dry. Remember to look after your crystals and they will look after you.

LIGHTING

Creative lighting can transform a dingy basement into an enticing den, and a boring store into a compelling attraction. It can be used to accentuate and focus attention, to lift and inspire, to activate and enhance. Install uplighting and downlighting to enrich selected areas of the bagua by illuminating plants, beautiful screens, and decorations. An attractive light outside your house is like a beacon to welcome you home. Use uplighting to raise oppressive energy such as low or sloping ceilings, and dull or cramped rooms or hallways. To correct a missing area, place a light in the far corner of it, aimed back toward the house.

Spotlight correcting a missing area

WIND CHIMES

I am always astonished at the number of times I go into people's homes and find wind chimes hanging in doorways or passageways so that you have to contort your body to get past them. Instead of enhancing the flow of energy, they are in fact obstructing it!

Wind chimes are mainly used in Feng Shui to moderate energy. Think of how it feels when you hold your hand up to the wind. If you hold your fingers together, the wind cannot pass through, but if you part your fingers, some of the wind will pass through the gaps. Wind chimes work the same way. They slow the energy by blocking some and allowing the rest to pass through. The beautiful tinkling chimes refine the energy as it passes. It is lovely to hear the chimes but not absolutely necessary to hear them for them to be effective, simply because they have been used for Feng Shui purposes for so many thousands of years that the energy they are connected to in the unseen realms will activate their function whether they are heard or not.

When would you need a wind chime? Well, if your stairs are directly in line with the front door, a wind chime hung from the ceiling somewhere between the bottom step and the door will moderate the rate at which energy (and, symbolically, money) tumbles down your stairs and escapes through the front door. If your front door is directly in line with your back door, you are likely to miss opportunities in life because the energy moves too quickly through your home, so a wind chime hung from the ceiling somewhere between the two will slow it down enough for you to get a look in. You can also hang one in a long passageway to moderate energy moving too fast, or place one in the relevant area of your bagua to soothe disruptive energy in that aspect of your life.

Another use of wind chimes is to raise the level of energy in a home. The Balinese love to hang bamboo wind chimes from the eaves of a building, and they have melodious *tingkliks* that rotate in the wind to produce delightful sounds that drift across rice fields. Chinese Feng Shui recommends hanging wind chimes near the entrance to a business to encourage trade.

PLANTS AND FLOWERS

Use plants that symbolically represent by their shape what you want to create. Generally speaking, round-leafed, upward-shooting plants work best in Feng Shui. One of my favorites is the Money Tree (*Crassula Argentea*, also known as the jade plant), which is excellent for enhancing Fortunate Blessings. Avoid spiky plants in confined areas because their cutting chi can result in arguments and irritation, especially if placed in the Relationships area.

One man who came to my "Getting Started with Feng Shui" workshop realized that he had had a collection of spiky cactus plants in the Fortunate Blessings corner of his house for the entire seventeen years that he had lived there. He got rid of them the day after the workshop. His wife, meanwhile, was visiting Singapore where his aunt lived, and she phoned to let him know that the aunt had spontaneously given them a check for a five-figure sum! The only other time she had given them a gift of money had been seventeen years earlier when they bought the house.

For more information about plants, see pages 191–92 and 198–99.

ANIMALS

Household pets can be very helpful in activating energy because they scamper around and keep it moving. After one little girl learned about the bagua, she enterprisingly put her hamster in the Fortunate Blessings area of her bedroom and encouraged it to run around and around its hamster wheel. She called me gleefully a few weeks later to let me know that her income from pocket money and other sources had tripled! Her hamster, unfortunately, had become exhausted and thin, and after discussing the matter she agreed that it would be better to settle for only double pocket money and a healthier hamster!

MOVING OBJECTS

Any moving object against a still background activates energy and draws attention. Flashing neon signs and other moving objects can be used in window displays to attract business. Escalators and moving walkways are also excellent, provided the number of down escalators does not exceed the number of those going up! In your home you can use mobiles to enhance whichever area of the bagua they are placed in.

SOLID OBJECTS

You can use objects such as stone statues as a Feng Shui cure to ground your energy (this is particularly useful if you sleep in a room with an unoccupied space below it). Other heavy objects made of wood or stone, or large items of furniture, can be used as a temporary enhancement to stabilize a situation such as a faltering career (place in the Journey area), finances (place in Fortunate Blessings), relationship (place in Relationships), and so on. Left too long these cures may have the opposite effect and cause the energy to stagnate, so do keep an eye on the situation.

SYMBOLIC OBJECTS

Use pictures and decorative objects in different areas of the bagua to symbolize what you want to create in each aspect of your life. One woman searching for her ideal partner had had a series of disappointing boyfriends. "They all needed firecrackers lighting under them to get them moving," she confided in me. Checking her home revealed a huge sedentary statue of a buddha ensconced in her Relationships area. She replaced it with a more active, macho figurine—and found her man!

As a Feng Shui cure for oppressive ceilings, use pictures of soaring balloons, kites, angels, helicopters, planes, birds, butterflies, and so on. Even flying ducks come into their own as a Feng Shui cure for a steep staircase (position them flying upward to help bring energy up the stairs).

W ·A T E R

I have yet to find a Chinese restaurant anywhere in the world where there is no aquarium or at least a picture of fish in water. Water activated by living fish is a well-known Chinese Feng Shui enhancement known to bring prosperity and is widely used by many businesses.

As a cure, fountains can be positioned between your home and a source of cutting chi in order to disperse it, and a birdbath placed in a missing area will attract high energy by bringing birds into the space.

C O L O R

Many years ago I lived in a big Victorian house and experimented with painting each of the rooms a different color. There was the Brown Room, the Red Room, and so on. I learned that each color has a very specific effect. Red activates and draws attention (notice how many stores use red in their logo). Blue cools and relaxes. Green heals and revitalizes. Yellow enriches the emotions. Brown is grounding but can be too heavy. Pink is the color of love. Orange stimulates hunger (don't paint your kitchen orange if you want to lose weight!).

White and black are not colors themselves, but the presence of all colors and the absence of all colors respectively. They symbolize different things in different cultures. For example, in Bali, white is the highest color and is the symbol of purity in the cycle of life and death; in China it is associated with death and mourning. White decor in a home can open up all possibilities, but too much white can indicate lack of purposeful direction. Black symbolizes the void of transition, and many teenagers go through a "black phase" (wearing black clothes, painting their rooms black, and so on) when they are finding themselves.

The use of colors is a huge topic with many personal factors to be taken into account. Colors, like smells, can stimulate memories buried deep in the subconscious mind and in the body. Dr. Max Lüscher, author of *The Lüscher Color Test*, became interested in establishing causes of color preference and conducted a very detailed study into the subject. He concluded that it was governed by "an existing state of mind or by a state of glandular balance."

The colors you see when you first enter your home condition the way you feel about being there and therefore what is possible for you in that space. Always choose colors that make you feel good.

Pastel colors have a higher vibrational rate than primary colors and are certainly best for babies' rooms. As they develop, most children become more attracted to primary colors. Allow them choice about the colors of their rooms when they get to an age where they start expressing preferences. Also become more aware of energy shifts in yourself that may alter the way you relate to the vibrational fields of different colors, and change your decor accordingly.

HOW DO YOU KNOW IF YOU HAVE GOT IT RIGHT?

Clicking

One very sensitive client said to me that as she went about her house making the changes I had suggested after an in-depth consultation, she could feel a distinct "click" inside her as she made each change. This is exactly right, because the whole art of Feng Shui is to redirect and realign energy flows. What she was actually experiencing was the "rightness" of the adjustment and the resonance inside her as the external change registered on an internal level.

How does it look?

Any Feng Shui changes you make should blend in with your home to enhance the way it looks. If guests walk into the place and say, "What on earth is that doing there?," you need to think again. Chinese mirrors and wind chimes may look great in Chinatown but can look very out-of-place in an elegant Western townhouse, so always use materials that go well with your own style of decor. If you have got it right, you will feel pleased with how it looks and others will compliment you on it.

How does it feel?

Your body knows exactly what is right for you and can be your greatest guide if you can learn to interpret its signals. Correct Feng Shui placement produces a feeling of joy and elation in the body, as well as a feeling of total comfort. Deepak Chopra describes this very well in his book *The Seven Spiritual Laws of Success*:

> There is a very interesting mechanism that the universe has to help make spontaneously correct choices. The mechanism has to do with sensations in your body. Your body experiences two kinds of sensations: one is a sensation of comfort, the other is a sensation of discomfort. At the moment you consciously make a choice, pay attention to your body and ask your body, "If I make this choice, what happens?" If your body sends a message of comfort, that's the right choice. If your body sends a message of discomfort, then it's not the appropriate choice.

Checking your breathing

We take energy into our bodies with every breath we take, and I explained in the early part of the book how important it is to breathe deeply and fully while you are Space Clearing in order to keep the energy moving. Similarly, when making Feng Shui changes in your home, your breath can be your guide to let you know if you have got it right. When the energy is flowing correctly, your breathing becomes easy and effortless. When the energy is constricted, you feel tight in the chest, and your breathing feels difficult. Learn to monitor your breathing to get clues as to how you are doing.

Is it producing results?

The real test for Feng Shui is: does your life work better as a result of it? Sometimes the changes happen dramatically and obviously, and I have given many such examples throughout the book. Other results happen more slowly or less obviously.

Very often people will say, "Ah, yes, but that might have happened anyway without the Feng Shui." Yes, it might, but then again it might not. I always remember one client who had an extraordinary run of wonderful "luck" after I advised her to hang a crystal in a certain window of her home. I went to visit her some time later, and she remained unconvinced that Feng Shui had anything to do with it. I offered to remove the crystal and reimburse her for it, but she sprang out of her chair and barred my way to the window. Her mind wouldn't admit it, but her body knew she needed to keep the crystal where it was!

These energy shifts sometimes have physical manifestations in your home. It sometimes happens after making Feng Shui adjustments that you get a few light bulbs burning out or the odd mechanical thing reacting. Machines that were unreliable can also "heal" themselves and start working better than before.

The thing to remember is that, as in many different forms of healing, things sometimes have to get worse in order to get better, in which case you simply need to hang in there for a little while and ride it out. However, if things repeatedly keep breaking down or you seem to be on a steep downward curve, then it is entirely possible that the Feng Shui adjustments are incorrect and need to be reversed. You may position a mirror with the best will in the world but may not realize that by doing so you have thrown something else completely out of balance.

If it ain't broke, don't fix it

In *Feng Shui Made Easy*, William Spear tells a cautionary tale of a man who implemented many Feng Shui changes around his home and suffered disastrous consequences. When he was questioned, it transpired that his life had been working excellently until then but by moving furniture and hanging crystals, wind chimes, mirrors, and so on to try to improve it further, he had disrupted the harmony he already had.

I have heard similar stories countless times. Don't be greedy! If your life is already working well, look around your home and learn from yourself. You will already have created a harmonious flow of energy in your space that is serving you well. A Feng Shui tweak here and there from time to time will be all you need.

20.

Integrating Feng Shui
into Your Life

Creating sacred space is about much more than creating your ideal home or workplace. It is about living consciously within the flow of universal energy from which all things manifest. It is about expanding your ability to give and receive love, your capacity for intimacy with people and things, your passion for life itself. It brings with it a new perception, new values, a whole new way of being and doing.

To successfully use the material in this book, the basic levels of Space Clearing, electromagnetic awareness, and Feng Shui need to become the focus of your attention for a while as you develop your skills and adjust your outer world to correspond to your inner aspirations. For some people this may be accomplished very quickly, for others more slowly. Be patient with yourself. Give yourself the time you need.

After creating your external environment as you want it, allow your focus to shift. Let Space Clearing and Feng Shui become part of the background support system in your life rather than the primary focus. Some people try to make a religion out of it. Others get so obsessed by it that they cannot make any changes in their home unless they check with their Feng Shui practitioner first. Realize that these tools are the means to an end, not the goal in itself. Integrate them into your way of life. Use them to empower yourself and gain mastery over your life.

We each have a responsibility to our Higher Self to create the neces-

sary circumstances on the physical plane to be able to fulfill our life purpose in coming here. Not to do so is to let ourselves down in this important part of our spiritual journey. By using Feng Shui to manifest our desires
in whatever form is meaningful to us, we walk a sacred path.

Remember also to always use these skills for the highest good of all,
never for purely selfish gain. In Bali they have a phrase, *gotong-royong*,
which roughly translates as "the spirit of mutual cooperation." Everyone
helps everyone, and everyone is helped by everyone. When you use Feng
Shui in this way, your life fills with love and abundance.

It has been my intention to write a book that has a positive transformational effect upon the lives of those who read it and put it into practice.
I believe that learning to create sacred space is immensely beneficial to all
our lives. I also believe that its effects resound farther than any of us can
know, like a domino effect around the universe. By taking responsibility
for purifying and refining our own atmospheres, improving the quality of
our electromagnetic environment, and harmonizing the energy flow
of our own spaces, we each make a significant contribution to the greater
good of all.

Bibliography and Recommended Further Reading

Clutter clearing

Kingston, Karen, *Clear Your Clutter with Feng Shui* (Broadway, 1999)
Treacy, Declan, *Clear Your Desk!* (Century Business, 1992)

Understanding energy

Sagan, Dr. Samuel, *Entity Possession: Freeing the Body of Negative Influences* (Destiny Books, 1997)

Geopathic stress and dowsing

Bachler, Käthe, *Earth Radiation* (Wordmasters Ltd, Manchester, England 1989)
Davidson, John, *Subtle Energy* (C. W. Daniel Co., 1993)
Gordon, Rolf, *Are You Sleeping in a Safe Place?* (The Dulwich Health Society, www.dulwichhealth.co.uk)

Lonegren, Sig, *Sig Lonegren's Dowsing Rod Kit* (Virgin Books, 1995)

Lonegren, Sig, *Spiritual Dowsing* (Gothic Image Publications, 1986)

Pohl, Gustav Freiherr von, *Earth Currents—Causative Factor of Cancer and Other Diseases* (Frech-Verlag, Germany, 1987)

Electromagnetic stress

Coghill, Roger W., *Something in the Air* (Coghill Research Laboratories, 1997)

Davidson, John and Lucie, *A Harmony of Science and Nature* (Wholistic Research Company, Cambridge, England, 1991)

London Hazards Center, *VDU Work and the Hazards to Health* (London Hazards Center Trust Ltd, 1993)

Powerwatch Network (a bimonthly newsletter available on subscription from 2 Tower Road, Sutton, Ely, Cambs CR6 2QA, England, website: www.powerwatch.org.uk)

Swartwout, Dr. Glen, *Electromagnetic Pollution Solutions* (Aerai Publishing, Hawaii, 1991)

The home

Christensen, Karen, *The Green Home* (Piatkus Books, 1995)

Day, Christopher, *Places of the Soul* (The Aquarian Press, 1990)

Martlew, Gillian and Shelley Silver, *The Green Home Handbook* (Fontana, 1991)

Pearson, David, *The Natural House Book* (Conran Octopus, 1994)

Venolia, Carol, *Healing Environments* (Celestial Arts, California, 1988)

Meditation and spirituality

Sagan, Dr. Samuel, *Awakening the Third Eye* (Clairvision, 1997)

Sagan, Dr. Samuel, *Atlantean Secrets* (4 volumes, Clairvision, 1999)

Metaphysics and healing

Chopra, Deepak, *The Seven Laws of Spiritual Success* (Amber-Allen Publishing and New World Library, 1994)

Edwards, Gill, *Living Magically* and *Stepping into the Magic* (Piatkus Books, 1991 and 1993)

Hay, Louise L., *You Can Heal Your Life* (Eden Grove Editions, 1988)

Liberman, Jacob, *Light Medicine of the Future* (Bear & Co. Publishing, Santa Fe, New Mexico, 1991)

Lüscher, M., *The Lüscher Color Test* (Washington Square Press, New York, 1969)

Sagan, Dr. Samuel, *Regression: Past-Life Therapy for Here and Now Freedom* (Clairvision, 1999)

Weeks, Nora, *The Medical Discoveries of Edward Bach, Physician* (The Dr. Edward Bach Healing Center, 1973)

Bali

Eiseman, Fred B., Jr., *Bali: Sekala and Niskala* (Periplus Editions, Singapore, 1990)

Budihardjo, Eko, *Architectural Conservation in Bali* (GadjahMada University Press, Yogjakarta, 1991)

Patra, Drs. Made Susila, *Hubungan Seni Bangunan dengan Hiasan dalam Rumah Tinggal Adati Bali* (PN Balai Pustaka, Bali, *1985*)

Colon cleansing

Gray, Robert, *The Colon Health Handbook* (Emerald Publishing, Nevada, 1980)

Jensen, Bernard, D. C., *Tissue Cleansing Through Bowel Management* (Bernard Jensen, California, 1981)

Sharan, Dr. Farida, *Herbs of Grace* (Wisdom Press, 1994)

How to Contact Karen Kingston

Karen Kingston's Website
www.spaceclearing.com

Karen Kingston's U.S. Office
P.O. Box 1189
Oceanside, CA 92054
Tel: Toll free (877) 91-SPACE or (760) 754 7012
Fax: (760) 754 7017
e-mail: USoffice@spaceclearing.com

Karen Kingston's U.K. Office
Suite 401, Langham House,
29 Margaret Street, London W1N 7LB, England
Tel/Fax: +44 (0)7000 772232
e-mail: UKoffice@spaceclearing.com

Karen Kingston's hotel in Bali
Dancing Dragon Cottages, Amed Beach, East Bali
www.dancingdragoncottages.com

All other inquiries
info@spaceclearing.com

Workshops, Professional Trainings, and Consultations

WORKSHOPS

The first three parts of this book form the companion volume to my most popular workshop, "Space Clearing." I also teach advanced levels of this workshop and other related subjects, primarily in the U.S.A., U.K., Australasia, and Europe. The high point of my teaching year is the Space Clearing workshops I lead in Bali. My international teaching schedule can be found at www.spaceclearing.com

PROFESSIONAL TRAINING COURSES

It is perfectly safe to space clear your own home using the information in this book exactly as it is presented but it is not designed for professional level use. Very few people in the world have the ability to hold the levels required to do this work professionally or the spiritual stamina to develop the necessary skills. It requires a minimum of ten years personal development work (twenty years is preferable) and a huge amount of very specific in-depth training.

I currently offer practitioner trainings in the U.S.A. and U.K. Details of these courses and prerequisites for applicants can be found at www.spaceclearing.com

PRIVATE CONSULTATIONS

I conduct Space Clearing, Clutter Clearing, and Feng Shui consultations around the world, and also have a directory of registered Space Clearing practitioners whom I have personally trained. To view this directory and find a practitioner near you, go to www.spaceclearing.com

Resources

Space Clearing equipment

My U.S. Office stocks the complete range of Space Clearing equipment—superb quality Balinese bells, harmony balls, Balinese altar cloths, and colorizers, recommended incenses, and much more. View the products online at www.spaceclearing.com or contact:

Karen Kingston's U.S. Office
P.O. Box 1189
Oceanside, CA 92054
Tel: Toll free (877) 91-SPACE or (760) 754 7012
Fax: (760) 754 7017
e-mail: USoffice@spaceclearing.com

Electromagnetic field detectors

Some types of electromagnetic field detectors sold to the general public are unreliable and/or do not measure the kinds of fields they claim to. Most types do not give the all-important separate readings for magnetic and electric components. I can highly recommend the equipment available from the following supplier, who ships postage free to the U.S.A. and offers a 10% discount if you mention my name when ordering:

Perspective Scientific Ltd
100 Baker Street, London W1M 1LA, England

Tel: +44 (0)20 7486 6837 / Fax: +44 (0)20 7487 3023
e-mail: sales@perspective.co.uk
Website: www.perspective.co.uk

Geopathic stress eliminators

Many people who have used the Raditech devices feel that they bring relief. They
are available from:

The Dulwich Health Society
130 Gypsy Hill, London Ei9 1PL, England
Tel: +44 8670 5883 Fax: +44 8766 8816
e-mail: info@dulwichhealth.co.uk
Website: www.dulwichhealth.co.uk

Colon cleansing herbs

It is essential that the colon cleansing is done with the guidance of an experienced
herbal practitioner. Dr. Christopher's herbal formulas can be obtained from:

HealthForce Regeneration Systems
P.O. Box 5005-29, Rancho Santa Fe, CA 92067-5005, U.S.A.
Tel: (800) 357 2717 (orders only)
Customer Service/Information Line: (619) 756 5292
Fax: (619) 756 9243
e-mail: orders@healthforce.net
Website: www.healthforce.net

Flower essences

These are widely available in alternative health stores. The best I have found are
the original remedies discovered by Dr. Edward Bach:

The Dr. Edward Bach Centre
Mount Vernon, Bakers Lane

Sotwell, Oxon OX10 0PZ, England
Tel: +44 (0)1491 834678
Website: www.bachcentre.com

Meditation and spirituality

In late 1999, I discovered an advanced school of meditation and spirituality based in Sydney, Australia, that I highly recommend. It runs courses in Australia and other parts of the world, including the U.S.A. and U.K., and is nonprofitmaking. The teachings of the founder, Dr. Samuel Sagan, are very compatible with my own.

Clairvision School
P.O. Box 33, Roseville, NSW 2069, Australia
Tel: +61 (0)2 9888 1999
e-mail: info@clairvision.org
Website: www.clairvision.org

Index

CLEAR YOUR CLUTTER
AND CHANGE YOUR LIFE

Clutter is stagnant energy. It clogs your home and your life. Clutter clearing is therefore essential to good Feng Shui. In her inspirational book, *Clear Your Clutter with Feng Shui*, Karen Kingston reveals the far-reaching effects of physical, mental, emotional, and spiritual clutter, and motivates you to clear it as never before. The ideal companion book to *Creating Sacred Space with Feng Shui*, this is an absolute must for pack rats and Feng Shui enthusiasts everywhere.